Gooseberry Patch co. ®

A Country Store In Your Mailbox ®

the Cozy home Cookbook

A Country Store In Your Mailbox®

Gooseberry Patch
600 London Road
Department BOOK
Delaware, OH 43015
★
1-800·854·6673

Copyright 1999, Gooseberry Patch 1-888052-36-8
Fifth Printing, September, 2001

How To Subscribe

Would you like to receive
"A Country Store in Your Mailbox"®?
For a 2-year subscription to our 96-page
Gooseberry Patch catalog, simply send $3.00 to:

Gooseberry Patch
600 London Road
Department BOOK
Delaware, OH 43015

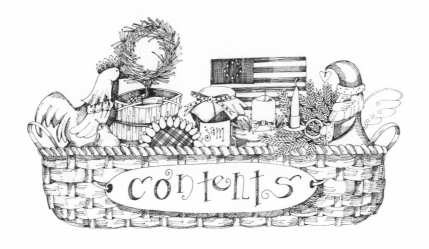

Contents

"Shut the door, not that it lets the cold in,
but that it lets the coziness out."
— Mark Twain

Dedication

For all who enjoy the simple pleasures
of "being home."

Appreciation

A heart-felt "thanks" to all who share the
warmth of their cozy homes with us.

Honey-Glazed Wings

Diane Chaney
Olathe, KS

Honey and ginger give these wings a wonderful sweet flavor.
Serve remaining marinade and your favorite blue cheese
dressing or honey mustard alongside for dipping!

1 c. soy sauce
1 c. green onions, chopped
8 T. white vinegar
3 T. honey
2 T. garlic, minced

2 T. fresh ginger, peeled and
  chopped
2 T. oil
20 chicken wings, tips removed

In a small mixing bowl, combine soy sauce, green onions, vinegar, honey, garlic, ginger and oil; whisking well. Add chicken wings, cover and chill 2 hours; stirring occasionally. Remove wings from marinade and place on 2 baking sheets; reserve marinade. Bake chicken wings in a 400 degree oven for one hour or until tender. Turn and baste with reserved marinade. Arrange wings on large platter. To prepare dipping sauce during last 5 minutes of baking time, place remaining marinade in a saucepan and bring to a boil until slightly thickened; stirring constantly. Remove from heat and place in a small bowl for serving.

✿ *Drape a pretty embroidered cloth on your outdoor table, add a centerpiece of flowers from your garden and invite friends over for a springtime tea!*

Cucumber-Dill Squares

Robin Wilson
Altamonte Springs, FL

One bite of these and you'll keep going back
for more...they're habit forming!

8-oz. pkg. cream cheese,
  softened
1-oz. pkg. Italian dressing mix

1 loaf pumpernickel bread, sliced
2 cucumbers, peeled and sliced
Garnish: fresh or dried dill weed

Mix cream cheese with Italian dressing mix; blend well. Spread cream cheese mixture on bread slices, top with a slice of cucumber and sprinkle dill weed on top. Refrigerate until ready to serve.

Rainbow Punch

Bonnie Egenton
Hillsborough, NJ

You can easily substitute your favorite color and flavor of gelatin.
If I'm serving this during the holidays, I'll use cranberry,
or lime for St. Patrick's Day!

6-oz. pkg. cherry gelatin
12-oz. can frozen lemonade
12-oz. can frozen orange juice

46-oz. can pineapple juice
2-ltr. bottle lemon-lime
  carbonated soda

Blend together gelatin, lemonade, orange juice and pineapple juice until gelatin is dissolved; stir in soda and serve.

He who plants a tree, plants love;
tents of coolness
spreading out above.

-Lucy Larcom

Creamy Fruit Ball

Julie Wise
Reynoldsburg, OH

This is a favorite recipe of mine to share at bridal showers; just serve with a variety of fresh fruit and gingersnaps or graham crackers.

2 8-oz. pkgs. cream cheese, softened
30-oz. can fruit cocktail, drained and diced

2 3-1/2 oz. pkgs. instant vanilla pudding
4 oz. pecans, ground

Mix cream cheese, fruit cocktail and pudding together into a ball. Roll in pecans until cheese ball is completely covered.

Banana Punch

Karen Moran
Navasota, TX

Our favorite punch for a crowd.

1-1/2 c. sugar
6 c. water
8 bananas
46-oz. can pineapple juice, divided

46-oz. can tropical punch
12-oz. can frozen orange juice
12-oz. can frozen lemonade
8 qts. ginger ale

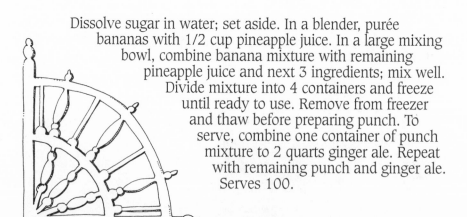

Dissolve sugar in water; set aside. In a blender, purée bananas with 1/2 cup pineapple juice. In a large mixing bowl, combine banana mixture with remaining pineapple juice and next 3 ingredients; mix well. Divide mixture into 4 containers and freeze until ready to use. Remove from freezer and thaw before preparing punch. To serve, combine one container of punch mixture to 2 quarts ginger ale. Repeat with remaining punch and ginger ale. Serves 100.

Appetizers

Strawberry-Lemon Fruit Dip

*Amy Blanchard
Ypsilanti, MI*

Strawberries and lemon together make a terrific light-tasting fruit dip! This is delicious on slices of pound cake, too.

8-oz. pkg. cream cheese,
  softened
1/2 c. sour cream
6 oz. lemon yogurt

1/4 c. strawberries, mashed
3 T. honey
1 T. maple syrup
fresh fruit

In a mixing bowl, beat cream cheese and sour cream until smooth. Add yogurt, strawberries, honey and syrup; mix well. Refrigerate at least 4 hours and stir well before serving. Makes 2 cups.

Sweet Brie Spread

*Rhonda Reeder
Ellicott City, MD*

Try this sweet spread with your favorite flavor of cream cheese!

3-oz. pkg. strawberry cream
  cheese, softened
8-oz. wheel of brie

gingersnap cookies
vanilla wafer cookies

Spread cream cheese over brie; refrigerate. Before serving, bring brie to room temperature then serve with gingersnaps or vanilla wafers.

Tap holes in the bottoms of unused watering cans, fill with dirt and flowers. They'll look so pretty lined along your steps or garden path!

9

Hawaiian Sweet Bread

Lisa Silver
Lamoni, IA

This recipe is an old-fashioned one, popular long before dough hooks or bread machines. The original recipe bears the stains of much use, and I hope your family likes it as much as ours does.

1 pkg. active dry yeast
1/2 c. plus 1 T. warm water,
   divided
1 c. milk
1/2 c. butter

1 c. sugar
1/2 t. salt
7 to 8 c. all-purpose flour,
   divided
5 eggs, divided

Dissolve yeast in 1/2 cup warm water; set aside. In a saucepan, combine milk, butter, sugar and salt; heat until warm, approximately 110 degrees. Remove from heat, place in a large mixing bowl and blend in yeast mixture. Stir in 4-1/2 to 5 cups of flour and mix well. Lightly beat 4 eggs and add to dough; mixture will be sticky. Set aside to let rise until double in bulk. Knead dough, adding enough remaining flour until dough is elastic and no longer sticky. Form into 2 round loaves and place in greased pie or round cake pans. Let rise again until double in bulk. Combine remaining egg and one tablespoon of water; beat well and brush over risen loaves. Bake at 350 degrees for 40 to 50 minutes.

❀ *Stencil your stairsteps! There are so many great country patterns...wreaths, pineapples, garlands or checkerboards look terrific in shades of barn red, mustard and navy.*

Breads

Cabinet Mountain Inn Rolls

Cindy Scott
Clark Fork, ID

In search of the perfect yeast rolls, a friend from Arkansas gave me a recipe. I made a couple of changes and truly found the taste I was looking for! These rolls are often found rising on the woodstove or on a sunny windowsill here at the inn.

2 pkgs. fast rising active yeast
2 c. warm water
1/2 c. sugar

1/2 c. shortening
1 t. salt
4 c. all-purpose flour

Dissolve yeast in water; set aside 10 minutes. Blend in sugar, shortening, salt and flour; knead well. Dough will be sticky, add more flour if needed. Place dough into a buttered pottery bowl, cover with a cloth and let rise in a warm place for one hour. Remove cloth, punch down dough and roll into 2-inch balls. Place one dough ball in each buttered cup in a muffin tin and let rise again for one hour or until dough has doubled in size. Bake at 375 degrees for approximately 15 to 20 minutes or until lightly golden. Makes 24 rolls.

Make your guest room welcoming. Fluffy pillows, a variety of books and magazines and a pitcher of cool water on the nightstand would make anyone feel extra special!

Chocolate Tea Bread

Pat Habiger
Spearville, KS

Applesauce is the secret ingredient that makes this cake-like loaf so moist! It's a success whenever I serve it.

1/2 c. applesauce
1/3 c. shortening
2 eggs
1/3 c. water
1-1/4 c. sugar
1-1/2 c. all-purpose flour
1/3 c. unsweetened cocoa

1 t. baking soda
3/4 t. salt
1/4 t. baking powder
6-oz. pkg. semi-sweet chocolate
   chips
1/3 c. walnuts

Combine applesauce, shortening, eggs, water and sugar; beat on low for 30 seconds. Combine dry ingredients; add to applesauce mixture. Beat on low for 30 seconds; beat on high for 2-1/2 minutes, scraping bowl occasionally. Fold in chocolate chips and nuts. Pour into a greased and floured 9"x5" loaf pan. Bake at 350 degrees for 60 to 70 minutes. Cool in pan 10 minutes before removing to a wire rack to cool completely. Drizzle with glaze.

Glaze:

1/2 c. powdered sugar
1 to 2 T. milk
1/4 t. vanilla extract

Blend ingredients; drizzle over bread.

Vintage iron hooks attached to a flea-market-find cornice, makes a handy hat rack!

Breads

Lemon-Poppy Seed Muffins

Zoe Bennett
Columbia, SC

So easy to make! These muffins are great for a springtime breakfast or brunch, served with fresh strawberries and chicken salad.

18-1/4 oz. pkg. white cake mix
6-oz. pkg. lemon pudding
2 T. poppyseeds

3 eggs
1-1/4 c. water
1/3 c. vegetable oil

In a large mixing bowl, blend together cake mix, pudding and poppy-seeds. In a separate bowl, combine eggs, water and oil until well blended. Blend into dry ingredients and gently stir. Line muffin tins with muffin cups, filling each cup about 2/3 full. Bake in a 350 degree oven for 20 minutes or until toothpick inserted into centers comes out clean. Cool 5 minutes before removing from muffin tin, then place on wire racks to cool completely. Makes 20 muffins.

❋ *A spring collection of straw bonnets, seed packets, old-fashioned watering cans and baskets of flowers will look cheerful sitting on your shelves. Change your collection with each season!*

Cream of Garlic Soup

Anna McMaster
Portland, OR

Serve this with a loaf of still-warm French bread and real butter. You could even top each serving with homemade croutons.

3/4 lb. ham, cubed
1 med. onion, chopped
10 garlic cloves, peeled and
   halved
2 lg. potatoes, peeled and cubed
2 T. butter

1/4 c. oil
6 c. chicken broth
1 c. whipping cream
1 c. half-and-half
salt and pepper to taste

Combine ham, onion, garlic and potatoes in a saucepan. Add butter and oil; sauté until onions are tender. Place in a large stockpot with chicken broth and cook one hour. Spoon broth mixture, a little at a time, into a blender and purée; repeat. Add purée to stockpot; blend in whipping cream and half-and-half. Heat through but don't boil. Season with salt and pepper. Serves 6.

❁ It's easy to create primitive kitchen cupboards! Just prime and paint, be sure to let each coat dry well, then sand off the edges where they would naturally wear. Lightly antique with brown stain, wipe off any excess and let dry.

Soups

Cabbage & Rice Soup

Kelly Alderson
Erie, PA

If you're short on time, prepare this soup up to 2 days in advance, refrigerate, then slowly reheat before serving.

3 T. garlic, minced
8 c. chicken broth, divided
1 c. long-grain white rice,
   uncooked

1-1/2 lb. cabbage head,
   shredded
salt and pepper to taste
Garnish: fresh parsley

Blend together garlic, 2 cups chicken broth and rice in a stockpot; bring to a boil. Reduce heat to a simmer and cook, covered, 20 minutes. Process rice mixture and 4 cups of broth in a blender; return to stockpot. Add remaining 2 cups broth and cabbage. Bring to a simmer for 15 minutes; season to taste. Garnish with parsley. Serves 6.

❀ *Begin a collection of all the things you love...birdhouses, crocks, cookie cutters, baskets, bobbins or pottery all make great country collections! You'll also have fun searching flea markets and tag sales for new items!*

Lemon-Chicken Soup

Kim McGeorge
Ashley, OH

Refreshing lemon adds just the right touch to a familiar favorite. A perfect soup for those days when there's just a little chill in the air.

10 c. chicken broth
3 celery stalks, sliced
3 lg. carrots, peeled and sliced
1 lg. onion, chopped
1 c. long-grain white rice, uncooked

1-1/2 lbs. boneless, skinless chicken breasts, chopped
3 lg. eggs, beaten
1/2 c. lemon juice
1 t. dried oregano

Combine broth, celery, carrots and onions in a large stockpot; bring to a boil. Add rice and chicken, simmer 15 minutes or until rice is tender. Combine eggs and lemon juice; gradually add to soup and stir with a fork until ribbons form. Sprinkle with oregano. Simmer 3 minutes before serving.

❀ *Almost anything can become a wonderful wreath for your door! Begin with a grapevine or straw base and use a glue gun to attach cookie cutters, birdhouses, tiny terra cotta pots and seed packets. Top your wreath off with a big raffia or homespun bow!*

Soups

White Cheddar-Asparagus Soup
Jo Ann

A great recipe for using the fresh, tender asparagus from your garden.

1-1/2 c. onion, chopped
1/2 c. butter
4 c. chicken broth
4 cubes chicken bouillon
3 potatoes, peeled and chopped
2 carrots, chopped
1 cauliflower head, cut into
    flowerets
2 broccoli bunches, cut into
    flowerets

1/2 c. rice, uncooked
3 c. asparagus, chopped
2 c. fresh spinach, torn
4 c. milk
salt and white pepper to taste
Garnish: 1/2 lb. white Cheddar
    cheese, shredded

Sauté onion in butter until tender. Transfer to a large stockpot and blend in broth, bouillon, potatoes, carrots, cauliflower, broccoli and rice. Simmer until rice is tender, approximately 15 to 20 minutes. Add asparagus and spinach to stockpot and return soup to a simmer. Blend in milk and continue to simmer over low until vegetables are crisp-tender. Season to taste with salt and pepper. Garnish with cheese. Serves 8.

❀ *You don't have to have an ordinary mailbox on your front porch! Search antique shops for vintage lunch pails, wooden candle boxes or lidded baskets with flat backs; they'll all look terrific!*

Three Pepper Pasta Salad

Donna Nowicki
Center City, MN

This is such a pretty pasta salad! Spoon it into a glass serving bowl and show off all the beautiful colors.

12-oz. pkg. tri-color spiral pasta
2/3 c. olive oil
3 T. red wine vinegar
1 T. dried basil
2 T. grated Parmesan cheese
1-1/4 t. salt
1/4 t. pepper

1 sm. red pepper, sliced
1 sm. green pepper, sliced
1 sm. yellow pepper, sliced
2-1/4 oz. can sliced black olives
2 T. green onions, sliced
8 oz. mozzarella cheese, cubed

Cook pasta according to package directions; drain and rinse with cold water. In a blender, process oil, vinegar, basil, Parmesan, salt and pepper until smooth. In a large serving bowl, combine pasta with peppers, olives, onions and oil mixture; toss to coat. Top with mozzarella and toss again.

❀ *Fill your kitchen windowbox with a miniature herb garden! You can pinch off fresh sage, oregano, basil or thyme whenever you need them!*

Salads

Springtime Salad

Megan Brooks
Antioch, TN

*Crisp spinach and fresh dill make this a favorite salad. Try it
topped with crumbled feta cheese or sunflower seeds.*

2-1/4 c. water
1/2 t. salt
10-oz. box couscous
3 T. lemon juice

6 T. olive oil
2 c. spinach, torn
1/4 c. green onion, chopped
3 T. fresh dill, finely chopped

Pour water into a saucepan, add salt and bring to a boil. Add couscous
and immediately remove pan from heat. Cover saucepan and let stand
5 minutes. Uncover, and toss couscous with a fork. Place in a serving
bowl; set aside. Blend lemon juice and oil together, toss with couscous
and let mixture cool completely. Toss couscous with spinach, green
onion and dill; refrigerate until thoroughly chilled. Serves 6.

*If you've collected several coverlets, layer them on top
of an old blanket chest. You'll enjoy seeing their
beautiful colors and patterns, and they'll be close at
hand to curl up in on a cool spring evening.*

Bowtie Tuna Salad

Lisa Rainero
Mount Pleasant, SC

A terrific salad for a family get-together or potluck.

16-oz. pkg. bowtie pasta
2 6-oz. cans tuna, drained
1/4 c. sweet onion, finely
   chopped
2 T. mayonnaise
2 T. mustard

salt and pepper to taste
2 lg. tomatoes, chopped
3 T. olive oil
2 T. balsamic vinegar
Garnish: tomato wedges

Cook pasta according to package directions. While pasta is cooking, prepare tuna salad. Drain tuna and mix with onion, mayonnaise, mustard, salt and pepper. Cut tomatoes into thin wedges. When pasta is cooked, drain; leave in colander and stir olive oil and vinegar in gently, allowing excess to drain. Divide pasta among 4 pasta bowls. Divide tuna salad into 4 portions and scoop into the middle of each pasta filled bowl. Garnish with tomato wedges around edge of bowl. Makes 4 servings.

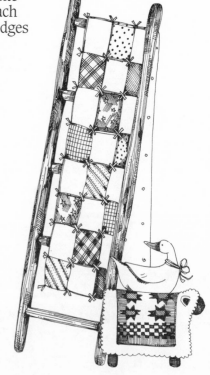

❀ Create a corner filled with nostalgia. Layer colorful quilts on an old wooden ladder, fill a cradle with stuffed toys and set a small table with your childhood tea set.

Salads

Petite Potato Salad

Gloria Kaufmann
Orrville, OH

This is our family's favorite potato salad recipe; my daughter served it at her wedding reception and it was a hit! We love it because it's almost more like an egg salad and everything is diced very small, that's why we call it petite!

3 med. potatoes, cooked and
    diced
salt and pepper to taste
10 hard-boiled eggs, diced
1 sm. onion, minced

2 bologna slices, diced
1/2 c. celery, diced
4 sweet pickles, diced
1/4 c. pickle juice

In a large serving bowl, combine potatoes with salt and pepper. Blend in remaining ingredients and lightly toss. Blend with one to 2 cups of dressing.

Dressing:

2 T. cornstarch
1-1/2 c. sugar
2 c. water
3 T. vinegar
1 t. salt

1 t. mustard
6 eggs, beaten
2 T. butter
1 qt. mayonnaise-style salad
    dressing

Combine cornstarch and sugar; gradually add water, stirring until smooth. Blend in next 3 ingredients. Add eggs to a double boiler and stir in cornstarch mixture. Cook over medium heat until mixture thickens, stirring constantly. Remove from heat, add butter and set aside to cool. Blend well with mayonnaise-style salad dressing and refrigerate. Makes 2 quarts.

Tomorrow when the wind is high, I'll build a kite to ride the sky!

-Rowena Bastin Bennett

Sweet & Tart Slaw

Joshua Logan
Corpus Christi, TX

Making your own cole slaw dressing is so easy with this recipe;
you won't believe how fresh it tastes!

2 c. red cabbage, shredded
2 c. green cabbage, shredded
1/2 c. carrot, grated
1 Granny Smith apple, sliced
1 c. raisins

1 c. mayonnaise-style salad
   dressing
1/2 c. sugar
1 T. white vinegar

Combine cabbage, carrot, apple and raisins in a large serving bowl; toss well. In a separate bowl, blend together remaining ingredients. Add desired amount of dressing to cabbage mixture, toss well to coat. Serve immediately. Makes 6 servings.

❀ *A springtime welcome! Hang a flower-filled basket on your garden gate. Wrap dried grapevine around the arbor to provide support for old-fashioned climbers like morning glories or sweet peas.*

Salads

Italian Garlic Salad

Phyllis Laughrey
Mount Vernon, OH

Serve with your favorite pasta dish!

1/2 c. olive oil
3 to 4 garlic cloves, minced
1-1/2 t. seasoned salt

2 iceberg lettuce heads, torn
Garnish: Gorgonzola or Feta
   cheese, crumbled

In a mixing bowl, combine olive oil, garlic and seasoned salt; whisk well. Toss with lettuce, top with desired amount of cheese.

Caesar Salad

Donna Knapp
Goodfield, IL

This tasty salad, a bowl of warm soup and some crusty rolls...a terrific light dinner!

1 garlic clove, crushed
1/3 c. olive oil
3 T. lemon juice
1 t. Worcestershire sauce
1/4 t. salt
1/4 t. dry mustard

pepper to taste
1 lg. Romaine lettuce bunch,
   torn
Garnish: 1 c. garlic croutons and
   1/2 c. fresh Parmesan
   cheese, grated

Whisk together garlic, oil, lemon juice, Worcestershire sauce, salt, mustard and pepper in a bowl. Add Romaine lettuce; toss until coated. Sprinkle with croutons and cheese.

Life begins the day you start a garden.
-Chinese Proverb

Spring Potluck Salad   *Vickie*

My favorite! It's all the yummy extras that make it so good!

2 oz. blue cheese
1/2 pt. strawberries, sliced
1 lettuce head, torn
1/2 c. walnuts
11-oz. can mandarin oranges

1 red onion, sliced
1/2 lb. bacon, crisply cooked
   and crumbled
balsamic or raspberry vinaigrette
Garnish: croutons

Combine blue cheese, strawberries, lettuce, walnuts, mandarin oranges, red onion and bacon; toss. Drizzle desired amount of vinaigrette over salad; toss to coat.

Croutons:

2 T. butter
2 t. olive oil

1 garlic clove, crushed
2 bread slices, crusts removed

Combine butter and oil together in a saucepan; stir until butter melts. Add garlic and cook over low heat until garlic is golden; remove from saucepan. Cut bread into 1/2-inch cubes and add to saucepan. As croutons become golden, turn with tongs and lightly brown on all sides. Set aside on a plate covered with paper towels. Repeat with any remaining bread cubes.

Salads

Sea Shell Salad

Amy Schwitters
Raymond, MN

You can substitute crab for the shrimp if you'd like, or use them both. Either way, it's a terrific seafood salad!

2 c. shell macaroni
2 T. onion, chopped
1 c. salad shrimp, cooked
3 celery stalks, chopped
1-1/2 c. carrots, grated
2 c. frozen peas

1 t. salt
1/4 t. garlic powder
3/4 c. mayonnaise-style salad
   dressing
1/2 c. French dressing
Garnish: shoestring potatoes

Cook shell macaroni according to package directions; drain. Combine with onion, shrimp, celery, carrots, peas, salt and garlic powder; toss well. In a small bowl, combine mayonnaise-style salad dressing and French dressing; blend well and toss with salad. Garnish with shoestring potatoes.

Wonderful welcomes! Stencil a wreath on your door or hang a straw hat tied with colorful ribbons. Pile the porch swing with pillows, hang a wind chime and don't forget the welcome mat! It's all the little touches that say "We're glad you stopped by!"

Parmesan Potatoes

Beth Hoffman
Santa Claus, IN

My family and I really enjoy this recipe; it's great and so easy!

1 stick margarine, melted
1 c. grated Parmesan cheese
1 c. all-purpose flour
2 t. salt

1 t. pepper
6 to 8 lg. potatoes, peeled and
    quartered

Place melted margarine into 13"x9" baking dish. Combine cheese, flour, salt and pepper in medium bowl. Dampen potatoes, roll in dry mixture and place in baking dish. Bake at 350 degrees for 30 minutes. Turn potatoes over, continue baking for an additional 30 minutes. Remove from oven, place potatoes in bowl and serve.

Springtime Asparagus

Jeannine English
Wylie, TX

Use fresh asparagus from your garden if you have it.

1-1/4 lbs. asparagus spears,
    ends trimmed
1 med. garlic clove, minced
1-1/2 t. fresh ginger, grated
1-1/2 t. rice wine vinegar
1-1/2 t. soy sauce

1 T. sesame oil
salt and pepper to taste
1 T. peanut butter
1 T. cilantro leaves, minced
1 T. water
Garnish: 1 med. scallion, minced

Steam asparagus until slightly tender, not entirely cooked. Combine garlic, ginger, rice wine vinegar, soy sauce and sesame oil, along with salt and pepper in a bowl. Brush asparagus with approximately one tablespoon of dressing. Broil for approximately 3 to 4 minutes or until asparagus is tender. Whisk together peanut butter, cilantro and water into remaining dressing; toss with asparagus. Transfer to a serving platter, sprinkle with scallion.

Sides

Fresh Tomato Pie

Julie Dobson
Loma Linda, CA

My grandmother shared this recipe with me; she really uses her talents to brighten the lives of those around her.

2 9-inch deep dish frozen pie
   crusts
3 T. butter
1 c. onion, chopped
1 c. green pepper, diced
1 garlic clove, minced
4 eggs

1 c. milk
1-1/2 c. Cheddar cheese,
   shredded
1-1/2 t. salt
1/4 t. pepper
2 med. tomatoes, sliced

Preheat oven to 325 degrees. Bake crusts in pie plates until golden. In medium skillet, melt butter and sauté onion, green pepper and garlic for 5 minutes. In medium bowl, lightly beat eggs. Stir in milk, cheese, salt, pepper and sautéed vegetables. Arrange an equal number of tomato slices in the bottom of pie crusts. Divide egg mixture in half and pour over tomatoes. Bake at 325 degrees for 50 minutes or until inserted knife comes out clean. Let pies stand at room temperature for approximately 15 minutes before cutting.

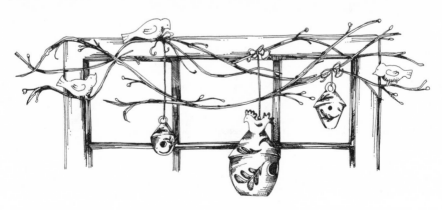

❀ *Grapevine makes a terrific window topper! Soak it in warm water until pliable, blot dry, then attach with small nails. Hang rusty tin stars, herbs or dried flowers from lengths of homespun or raffia.*

Spring Peas & Artichokes

Tina Wright
Atlanta, GA

Two of the best spring vegetables combined!

5 lbs. artichokes
1/4 c. lemon juice
1 lb. fresh peas, shelled
1 T. sugar
1-1/2 c. olive oil

3 garlic cloves, minced
1 T. salt
1/2 t. crushed red pepper flakes
1/2 c. water

Remove tough outer artichoke leaves and stem; set aside. Pour lemon juice into a large mixing bowl; fill bowl with cold water. Slice artichokes in half and place in lemon water. Place peas in a saucepan, cover with water and stir in sugar. Bring to a boil and cook 5 to 7 minutes, until peas are crisp-tender; drain and set aside. Pour olive oil in a skillet over medium-high heat. Add garlic and sauté one minute. Remove artichokes from lemon water, drain and add to skillet; sprinkle with salt. Cover skillet and cook 5 minutes, stirring occasionally. Blend in red pepper flakes and stir well. Cook one minute then add water. Cover and continue cooking. After 5 minutes, remove lid and reduce heat to medium and continue to cook and stir for another 5 minutes. Blend in peas and cook 3 minutes longer or until peas are heated through. Serves 8.

Happiness sneaks in through a door you didn't know you left open.

-John Barrymore

Sides

Dilly Cauliflower

Stephanie Mayer
Portsmouth, VA

A quick recipe for a family picnic!

1 head cauliflower, cut into
    flowerets
1 t. Dijon mustard
1 T. balsamic vinegar
1 T. lemon juice

1 green onion, chopped
2 T. fresh dill, minced
2 T. olive oil
salt and pepper to taste
Garnish: 1/2 c. walnuts, chopped

Place cauliflower in a steamer or in a colander set inside a saucepan of boiling water. Cover and steam cauliflower until tender. In a mixing bowl, combine mustard, vinegar, lemon juice, onion, dill, olive oil, salt and pepper; whisk well. Place cauliflower in a serving bowl and toss with dressing. Garnish with walnuts.

Place your favorite collectibles in unexpected places! Primitive wooden cutouts and gameboards look great hanging over doorways or windows, favorite teacups can hold pretty handmade soaps, crocks look great on a desk filled with paperclips or pencils.

Creole Green Beans

Cheryl Chapman
Union, MO

A wonderful green bean side dish; a twist on the usual recipe!

6 bacon slices, crisply cooked
  and crumbled, drippings
  reserved
1/4 c. onion, chopped
1/2 c. green pepper, chopped
2 T. all-purpose flour
2 T. brown sugar, packed

1 T. Worcestershire sauce
1/2 t. salt
1/4 t. pepper
1/8 t. dry mustard
16-oz. can peeled whole
  tomatoes
16-oz. can green beans, drained

Combine onion and green pepper in skillet with bacon drippings; sauté until tender. Blend together flour, sugar, Worcestershire sauce, salt, pepper and mustard; stir into skillet. Add tomatoes and continue to stir until mixture thickens. Add green beans and heat through; sprinkle with crumbled bacon.

❀ *Enjoy the coziness of your fireplace even when it's not in use. Set a basket in the opening and fill it with lots of canning jars or milk bottles overflowing with fresh flowers!*

Sides

New England Beans & Rice

The Governor's Inn
Ludlow, VT

Here at the inn we're constantly searching for new ways to present "New England" to our guests. We came up with this recipe which is a little different, but uses familiar ingredients. We think it's always a nice surprise tucked into a picnic basket.

6 maple-flavored bacon slices
1 c. onion, chopped
1/2 c. catsup
6 T. brown sugar, packed
1 T. Dijon mustard

3/4 t. salt
pepper to taste
3 c. white rice, cooked
2 15-oz. cans pinto beans, drained

In a large skillet with deep sides, fry bacon until it's half cooked; set aside. Add onions to bacon drippings, sauté until tender but not browned. Stir in remaining ingredients; mixing well. Pour into a buttered 15"x10" baking pan. Arrange reserved bacon slices on top. Bake at 350 degrees for 45 minutes. Serves 12.

A cheerful greeting...paint or stencil your mailbox, then attach a planter to the wooden post and fill with cascading flowers!

Rosemary Chicken

Robbin Chamberlain
Worthington, OH

Sprigs of fresh rosemary and lemon give this dish a light,
refreshing taste for spring suppers.

4 boneless, skinless chicken
   breasts
1/2 c. lemon juice
1/4 c. sherry

1 t. lemon zest
2 T. honey
3 T. fresh rosemary sprigs

Clean, dry and flatten chicken between 2 pieces of plastic wrap.
Marinate chicken in remaining ingredients for several hours. Remove
from marinade and place in a 2-quart baking dish. Bake, covered, at
375 degrees for 30 minutes. Remove cover and bake an additional
20 minutes. Remove rosemary sprigs before serving. Serves 4.

Roast Tenderloin of Beef

The Governor's Inn
Ludlow, VT

Here's our favorite recipe for the best roast!

2-lb. tenderloin of beef, trimmed
1/2 c. lemon juice

3 T. pepper

Pat roast dry, then, using lengths of white cotton butcher twine, tie
tenderloin together at 4 inch intervals. Roll the beef in lemon juice and
then in pepper until completely covered. Allow beef to stand until it is
room temperature, and place in a roasting pan. Bake at 500 degrees
for 32 minutes; one minute per ounce if you have a smaller or larger
roast. Remove from oven, loosely cover with aluminum foil and allow
to rest for 20 to 30 minutes before slicing. Serves 6.

The most beautiful place on earth,
our childhood home.

—Peggy Jones

Three Cheese Garden Pizza

Kathy Achen
Las Cruces, NM

Loaded with fresh vegetables!

10-oz. pkg. refrigerated pizza
   dough
2 garlic cloves, pressed
1 c. mozzarella cheese, shredded
1 c. Cheddar cheese, shredded
1 med. tomato, sliced

1 med. zucchini, sliced
1 sm. onion, sliced
1 c. mushrooms, sliced
1/4 c. grated Parmesan cheese
1 t. dried Italian seasoning

Roll out dough, place on a cookie sheet or pizza pan and bake at 400 degrees for 7 minutes. Spread garlic over crust and sprinkle cheeses evenly over top. Layer on vegetables, top with Parmesan cheese and sprinkle with Italian seasoning. Bake 15 to 18 minutes or until crust is golden and cheese is melted.

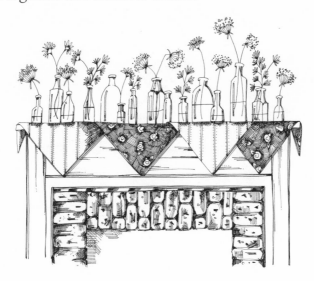

❀ *Layer vintage handkerchiefs on your mantel, letting them fall over the edge. Tuck fresh flowers in old-fashioned milk bottles, cobalt blue jars or teacups; a fragrant way to welcome spring!*

Chicken-Mushroom Fettuccine

Cathy Hillier
Salt Lake City, UT

Quick to make, this is wonderful served with a crisp Caesar salad.

1 t. oil
1-1/2 c. mushrooms, sliced
1/2 c. onion, chopped
1 garlic clove, minced
1 lb. skinless, boneless chicken
    breasts, sliced
salt and pepper to taste

1/2 t. dried basil
2 c. tomato, chopped
4 c. fettuccine, cooked
Garnish: 1/4 c. fresh Parmesan
    cheese, grated

Add oil to a large skillet. Over medium-high heat, combine mushrooms, onion and garlic; sauté 2 minutes. Stir in chicken, salt, pepper and basil. Sauté 5 minutes or until chicken is no longer pink and juices run clear. Blend in tomato; sauté 2 minutes longer. Serve over prepared pasta; garnish with cheese. Serves 4.

❀ *If you're lucky to have exposed beams in your home, show off a few of your favorites... crocks, pottery, baskets or punched tin. Each time you look at them they'll bring back fond memories of where you found them or who gave them to you.*

Asparagus Quiche

Marla Arbet
Burlington, WI

Our family really enjoys this! It's a change from the more traditional quiche recipes and the mix of cheeses gives it such a good flavor.

9-inch pie crust, baked
8 bacon slices, crisply cooked
   and crumbled
1 c. Swiss cheese, grated
1 c. Fontaine cheese, grated
10 asparagus spears, cooked
   and chopped

3 eggs
1-1/2 c. half-and-half
1 T. ground mustard
1/8 t. cayenne pepper
1/8 t. pepper

Crumble bacon evenly in bottom of pie crust. Sprinkle cheeses and asparagus on top. Mix eggs, half-and-half, mustard and peppers; blend well and pour over cheese and asparagus. Bake at 375 degrees for 45 minutes. Let stand 15 minutes before slicing.

To decorate an ordinary flower pot, you don't have to be an artist! Have fun painting a primitive farm scene on a terra cotta pot; add a checkerboard border around the rim. After the paint has dried, give it an antique look by wiping on stain, then protect it with a clear matte sealer.

Paprikash Chicken

Wendy Paffenroth
Pine Island, NY

For 20 years I'd heard about a great paprika chicken dish my husband's mom made, but when she passed away, there wasn't any written recipe. One day I searched through dozens of cookbooks and came up with this recipe...a combination of many different ones! My husband says this is a keeper!

1/3 c. all-purpose flour
1 t. pepper
1 T. paprika
1/8 t. salt
1 T. dried parsley
6 skinless chicken breasts

1/2 c. vegetable oil
1 onion, sliced in rings
2 chicken bouillon cubes
3 c. hot water
1 c. sour cream
Garnish: paprika

In a gallon plastic bag, place flour, pepper, paprika, salt and parsley. Rinse chicken and coat in flour mixture. In a large skillet, heat oil and brown each chicken piece. Place each piece in a 13"x9" baking dish. Brown the remaining flour with onion, bouillon and water; bring to a boil. Pour half of this mixture over the chicken; reserve remaining half. Bake, covered, at 350 degrees for 35 minutes; remove and drain. Heat, but do not boil, reserved sauce, and add sour cream. Serve chicken over noodles. Spoon sauce over top and garnish with paprika.

Create a country window topper in no time. Attach small birdhouses to the corners of your window, then string a garland between them; so easy!

Vegetable Lasagna

Michelle Urdahl
Litchfield, MN

A lighter version of an old favorite!

10 lasagna noodles
2 T. butter
2 c. mushrooms, sliced
1 sm. onion, chopped
1 garlic clove, minced
2 T. all-purpose flour
1 t. pepper
1-1/4 c. milk
2 10-oz. pkgs. frozen, chopped
spinach, thawed and drained
1 med. carrot, shredded

3/4 c. Parmesan cheese,
shredded
2 eggs, beaten
2 c. cottage cheese
2 c. ricotta cheese
1-1/2 t. dried Italian seasoning,
crushed
8-oz. pkg. mozzarella cheese,
shredded, divided

Cook noodles according to package directions; drain and set aside. Melt butter in a saucepan, stir in mushrooms, onion and garlic and sauté until tender. Stir in flour and pepper. Blend in milk, stir well and continue to cook until thick and bubbly. Cook and stir one minute more; remove from heat. Add spinach, carrot and 1/2 cup of Parmesan cheese. In a separate mixing bowl, combine eggs, cottage cheese, ricotta cheese and Italian seasonings. In an oiled 3-quart rectangular baking dish, layer the following in order; 1/3 of the noodles, 1/3 of the cottage cheese mixture, 1/3 of the spinach mixture, 1/3 of mozzarella cheese. Repeat the layers 2 more times and sprinkle with remaining 1/4 cup Parmesan cheese. Bake, uncovered, at 350 degrees for 35 minutes or until heated through. Let stand 10 minutes before cutting.

Sandy's Chocolate Eclair

Phyllis Stout
East Palatka, FL

*When I make this recipe, I always think of my aunt Sandy
and how lucky I am to have her in my family.*

2 3-oz. pkgs. instant vanilla
   pudding
3 c. milk

8 oz. whipped topping
16-oz. box graham crackers

Mix pudding with milk. When it starts to thicken, fold in whipped topping. Line a 13"x9" pan with one layer of graham crackers. Pour half of the pudding mixture over the crackers, add an additional layer of crackers on top of the pudding; then pour the remaining pudding on top. To this layer of pudding, finish with a third layer of crackers and cover with chocolate icing. Pour icing over cracker-pudding mixture. Refrigerate overnight to soften crackers. Makes 6 to 8 servings.

Icing:

1/3 c. butter, softened
1/2 c. cocoa

2 c. powdered sugar
4 T. milk

In medium bowl, mix together butter, cocoa, powdered sugar and milk.

❀ *A sure sign of spring!
Use birdhouses as cheerful
centerpieces for your
picnic table, or group
them together on
windowsills, cupboard
shelves or mantels!*

Desserts

Chocolate Chip-Molasses Cookies

Laura Jacquin
New Haven, MO

This recipe was given to me by my mother-in-law and proved to be the key to my husband's heart...bake them with love.

1 c. sugar
1/2 c. shortening
1 egg
1/2 c. molasses
2 c. all-purpose flour
1 t. salt

1-1/2 t. baking soda
1 t. vanilla extract
1 c. quick cooking oats
12-oz. pkg. semi-sweet
chocolate chips

Cream sugar and shortening, add egg and molasses; beat well. Add sifted dry ingredients, mix well. Add vanilla, then stir in oats and chocolate chips. Place in greased 13"x9" cake pan. Bake 25 minutes in a 350 degree oven. When cool, cut into squares. Makes 32.

Easter Eggs

Elizabeth Blackstone
Racine, WI

The perfect homemade treat to tuck in all your baskets!

3-oz. pkg. cream cheese,
softened
3-1/2 c. powdered sugar
4 drops almond extract

food coloring
multicolored sprinkles
chocolate sprinkles

Cream together cream cheese and powdered sugar; mix well. Blend in almond extract and a few drops of food coloring. Continue to blend together until food coloring is well combined. Using your hands, shape mixture into egg shapes then roll in sprinkles. Chill in refrigerator until ready to serve.

Teatime Cookies

Tina Stidam
Delaware, OH

Plan a "girls only" tea on your porch this spring!

1 c. butter, divided
3/4 c. sugar, divided
4 eggs, separated and divided
1/4 c. plus 1 to 2 T. lemon juice, divided

1 T. plus 2 t. lemon zest
2 c. all-purpose flour
1/8 t. salt
powdered sugar

Make lemon curd by combining 1/4 cup butter and 1/4 cup sugar in the top of a double boiler. Simmer until butter melts. Blend together one egg, 2 egg yolks, 1/4 cup lemon juice and one tablespoon lemon zest; whisk into butter and sugar mixture. Whisk until mixture thickens; do not boil. Remove double boiler from heat and allow to sit 5 minutes, cover and refrigerate until well chilled. To make cookies, cream together remaining butter and sugar. Blend in one egg yolk and remaining lemon zest. Mix flour and salt together then stir into butter mixture; beat in one tablespoon lemon juice. If dough feels dry, add lemon juice until dough is smooth. On a lightly floured surface, roll dough 1/8-inch thick and cut with your favorite cookie cutters. Bake at 350 degrees on a lightly oiled cookie sheet for 6 minutes or until lightly golden; cool on a wire rack. After cookies have cooled, remove lemon curd from refrigerator. Sandwich cookies together by spooning enough lemon curd on the bottom of one cookie to "glue" it to another cookie placed on top. Sprinkle with powdered sugar. Makes 5 dozen cookies.

❀ *Who doesn't remember little girl tea parties and playing dress-up? A vintage tea cart is the perfect place for displaying grandma's teapot, teacups and china...a sweet memory.*

Desserts

Carrot Cake

Julie Hogan
Cornwall, VT

A family favorite! It's crunchy on the outside and moist in the middle!

1-1/2 c. vegetable oil
2-1/2 c. sugar
4 eggs, separated and divided
5 T. hot water
2-1/2 c. all-purpose flour
1-1/2 t. baking powder
1/2 t. baking soda

1/4 t. salt
1 t. nutmeg
1 t. cinnamon
1 t. cloves
1-1/2 c. carrots, grated
1 c. walnuts, chopped

Grease and flour a 10" tube pan. Cream oil and sugar. Beat in egg yolks one at a time. Beat in hot water. Sift flour with other dry ingredients and beat into egg mixture. Stir in carrots and nuts. In a separate bowl, beat egg whites until stiff peaks form and fold into cake mixture. Bake at 350 degrees for 60 to 70 minutes. Cool 15 minutes in pan and then remove. Cool and frost with cream cheese frosting. Makes about 16 servings.

Cream Cheese Frosting:

3-oz. pkg. cream cheese
1/4 c. margarine

1 t. vanilla extract
2-1/4 c. powdered sugar

Cream together cream cheese, margarine and vanilla until light and fluffy. Add one cup powdered sugar; beating well. Beat in about 1-1/4 cups more powdered sugar to make a spreading consistency.

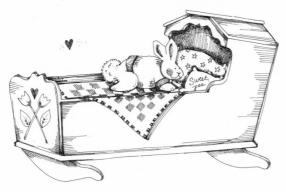

Auntie Mayme's Rhubarb Custard Pie
Mary Terdich
Crystal Lake, IL

*A delightful family recipe handed down from my husband's aunt.
It's smooth, creamy and delicious!*

1/3 stick butter
1-1/4 c. sugar
3 c. rhubarb, chopped
4 T. cornstarch
6 T. water, divided

2 egg yolks, beaten
1 t. vanilla extract
9-inch pie crust, baked
Garnish: whipped topping

Melt butter in a saucepan, add sugar and stir in rhubarb. Cook over medium heat until tender and smooth. Combine cornstarch, 3 tablespoons water; mix. Beat egg yolks and remaining water together. Blend in vanilla and add to cooled rhubarb. Heat over low temperature and cook until thick. Pour into pie crust and top with whipped topping if desired. Chill.

❀ *A country welcome!
Fill baskets, crocks, sugar
buckets and galvanized
tubs with flowers and
herbs. If you want a
really old-fashioned
touch in your garden, add
a weathered rain barrel
to catch rain water...
it's so handy and great for
watering your plants!*

Layered Lemon Dessert

Laura Perez
Goliad, TX

Great with a cup of chamomile tea.

10 T. butter, divided
1-1/2 c. all-purpose flour
1-1/2 c. pecans, finely chopped
8-oz. pkg. cream cheese,
    softened
1-1/2 c. powdered sugar
1-1/2 c. whipped topping
2 c. sugar

1/3 c. cornstarch
1/4 t. salt
2 c. water, divided
3 eggs
1/4 c. vinegar
1/4 c. lemon juice
1 t. lemon extract

Cut 9 tablespoons butter into flour until crumbly. Stir in pecans and press into the bottom of an ungreased 13"x9" baking pan. Bake at 350 degrees for 15 minutes; cool. Beat cream cheese and powdered sugar until fluffy. Fold in whipped topping. Spread over crust; chill. In a saucepan, combine sugar, cornstarch and salt. Add 1/4 cup water and stir until smooth. Add eggs and mix well. Add vinegar, lemon juice and the remaining water; stir until smooth. Bring to a boil over medium heat, stirring constantly; boil for one minute. Remove from heat; add remaining butter and extract. Cool and spread over cream cheese layer. Chill at least 2 hours or overnight.
Serves 12 to 16.

Spring

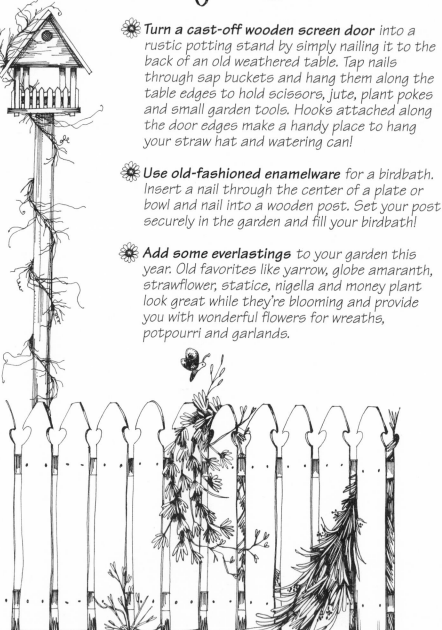

Turn a cast-off wooden screen door into a rustic potting stand by simply nailing it to the back of an old weathered table. Tap nails through sap buckets and hang them along the table edges to hold scissors, jute, plant pokes and small garden tools. Hooks attached along the door edges make a handy place to hang your straw hat and watering can!

Use old-fashioned enamelware for a birdbath. Insert a nail through the center of a plate or bowl and nail into a wooden post. Set your post securely in the garden and fill your birdbath!

Add some everlastings to your garden this year. Old favorites like yarrow, globe amaranth, strawflower, statice, nigella and money plant look great while they're blooming and provide you with wonderful flowers for wreaths, potpourri and garlands.

Spring

❀ **Make a garland of daisies!** String it across your garden gate or around a birdhouse...lovely!

❀ **Bundle up bunches of Sweet Annie,** tie with raffia and hang them on your fence posts or gate. Every time you brush against them, they'll release a sweet fragrance.

❀ **Hang an old-fashioned straw hat** on your gate. Secure it with lots of colorful ribbons...they'll look beautiful blowing in the breeze!

❀ **Paint a garden pail!** Prime a metal pail with spray metal primer; let dry. Paint your favorite design on with gloss acrylic paints and when the paint's dry, coat the pail with a clear enamel sealer. Hang it near your garden to hold small gardening tools or a bouquet of just-picked flowers!

Kites ❦ Strawberries ☂ Rain
daisies & daffodils
caterpillars fresh
grass Teacups ❦ New beginnings
Bows Rainbows Tulips eggs Cleaning

Garlic & Chive Cheese Spread

Kathy Solka
Ishpeming, MI

Make this spread low calorie; just substitute fat-free cream cheese and ricotta...it's equally as good!

8-oz. pkg. cream cheese,
    softened
1 c. ricotta cheese
2 garlic cloves, minced
2 T. chives, minced

1 t. dried thyme
1 t. dried oregano
1 t. Worcestershire sauce
hot pepper sauce to taste

Combine all ingredients, blending well. Serve with fresh vegetables, bread sticks or assorted crackers.

Tea Julep

Barb Bargdill
Gooseberry Patch

A refreshing summer drink!

2 c. cold water
1/2 c. sugar
1/2 c. fresh mint leaves,
    lightly packed

7 c. tea, brewed and chilled
Garnish: 8 sm. mint sprigs

In a small saucepan, combine water, sugar and mint. Stir over low heat until sugar is dissolved. Increase heat to medium and bring to a boil; boil about 5 minutes or until liquid is slightly syrupy. Remove from heat and set aside to cool. Strain into a bowl or pitcher; stir in tea. Pour into ice filled glasses and garnish with mint sprigs. Makes 8 servings.

East or West; home is best.

–Dutch proverb

✨ Appetizers ✨

Grandma's Deviled Eggs

Vicki Lane
Valley Center, CA

This recipe has been in our family for generations...my grandma remembers her grandmother making them. When I was a young girl, Grandma would teach me to cook and this was my favorite. It's never been written down until now. Each time I make it, I lovingly remember all the special times I spent in the kitchen with Grandma.

20 eggs, hard-boiled	2 T. sugar
6 to 8 T. mayonnaise	1/2 t. salt
1 T. mustard	1/2 t. pepper
1 T. vinegar	Garnish: paprika

Cool and peel eggs; cut in half, lengthwise. Place egg yolks into a bowl and place whites on a serving dish. Mash egg yolks with a pastry blender or a fork then blend in remaining ingredients; mix until smooth. Spoon mixture into the egg whites and sprinkle with paprika. Refrigerate until ready to serve. Makes 40 deviled eggs.

☆ *Stitch together old-fashioned flour and sugar sacks and stuff with polyester fiberfill...they'll look great tossed on a porch swing or in your rocking chair!*

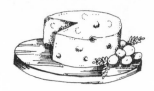

Hot Virginia Dip

Debi Gilpin
Bluefield, WV

Shared with me by a friend at church, this dip is really good!

8-oz. pkg. cream cheese,
  softened
1/2 c. sour cream
2 T. milk
2-1/2 oz. jar dried beef, chopped

1/3 c. green onion, chopped
3 T. green pepper, chopped
1 T. pimento, chopped
1/8 t. pepper
1/4 c. pecans, chopped

Combine cream cheese, sour cream and milk; blend well. Add next
5 ingredients; mix well. Spoon into an 8" baking dish and sprinkle
with pecans. Bake at 350 degrees for 15 to 20 minutes.

Strawberry-Watermelon Slush

Sandy Benham
Sanborn, NY

On a hot summer day, this will quench your thirst!

1 pt. fresh strawberries, halved
2 c. watermelon, seeded and
  cubed

1/3 c. sugar
1/3 c. lemon juice
2 c. ice cubes

Mix first 4 ingredients together in a blender; blend until smooth.
Gradually add ice and continue to blend. Serve immediately.
Makes 5 cups.

*Ah! There is nothing like staying at
home for real comfort.*

-Jane Austin

Veggie Puffs

*Marissa Charyton
North Bellimore, NY*

*You can also fill these with sweet potato, cheese,
or try any of your favorite fillings!*

10 4-inch squares puff pastry dough
1-1/2 to 2 c. frozen mixed broccoli, carrots and cauliflower
3 egg whites, divided

1/4 c. mozzarella cheese, shredded
1/4 c. Cheddar cheese, shredded
1/8 t. dried basil
Garnish: sesame seeds

Defrost puff pastry dough squares for 5 to 10 minutes. Cook vegetables according to package directions; mash. Beat 2 egg whites and add to vegetables. Blend in cheeses and basil; mix well. Place one tablespoon filling in the center of each dough square. Fold dough to form triangles. Using the tines of the fork, seal edges of the dough. Lightly beat the third egg white and brush the top of the dough; sprinkle with sesame seeds. Place on a lightly oiled baking sheet and bake at 375 degrees for 10 to 12 minutes.

☆ Add whimsy to your garden shed! The sprinkling head from a watering can makes a fun door knob and an old trowel can become a clever door knocker!

Bacon & Herb Clams

Geneva Rogers
Gillette, WY

Have a clam bake this summer! It's a great way to have fun and catch up with friends and family. Start things off by serving these tempting appetizers.

4 bacon slices, crisply cooked
  and crumbled, drippings
  reserved
3 T. onion, chopped
3 T. green pepper, chopped
3 T. red pepper, chopped
2 t. Worcestershire sauce
1/2 t. dried thyme

1/2 t. dried marjoram
1/2 t. pepper
1/4 t. dried oregano
1/4 t. garlic salt
2 sticks butter, softened
16 clams on the half shell
1/3 c. dry bread crumbs

In a medium saucepan, combine one tablespoon reserved bacon drippings with onion, peppers, Worcestershire sauce and seasonings. Over medium heat, sauté until vegetables are tender; remove from heat and set aside to cool. Using an electric mixer, blend softened butter; stir into vegetable mixture. Spoon one tablespoon of vegetable mixture on each clam; top with bread crumbs. Bake at 450 degrees for 10 minutes or until bubbly.

☆ Create a summer nook full of memories. Dress up a tabletop with seashells the kids collected at the beach and family photos that captured all the fun!

✯∴ Appetizers ∴✯

Roast Beef Wraps

Nancy Wise
Little Rock, AR

Quick to make and great for picnics!

1 c. sour cream
2 T. horseradish
1 T. Dijon mustard
5 8-inch flour tortillas

30 fresh spinach leaves, stems
  removed
10 roast beef slices
1 c. Cheddar cheese, shredded

Combine sour cream, horseradish and Dijon mustard; blend until creamy. Spread mixture equally on each tortilla and layer on several spinach leaves. Place 2 slices of roast beef over spinach; sprinkle on cheese. Fold opposite edges of the tortilla toward the center over the filling then begin rolling one of the open ends toward the opposite edge, rolling tightly. Refrigerate 2 hours. Before serving, slice each tortilla into 2-inch pieces or in half for larger appetizers.

☆ All of your favorite summertime delights can
be displayed on your mantel...sailboats, watering cans,
birdhouses, small gardening tools
and terra cotta pots.

Garden Patch Bread

Beth Prukop
Inez, TX

The freshest garden vegetables make this handy
bread machine recipe even better!

1 c. warm water	2 to 3 c. bread flour
1/3 c. tomato juice	3/4 t. sugar
1 c. carrot, shredded	1/2 t. salt
1/4 c. green pepper, chopped	1/4 t. dried basil
1/4 c. onion, chopped	1 t. yeast

To make a 1-1/2 pound loaf of bread, place all ingredients in your bread machine in the order the manufacturer suggests. Add enough bread flour so dough doesn't stick to the sides of the machine and bake according to manufacturer's instructions.

☆ Remember the fun of making daisy chains? Gather together a string of black-eyed Susans, daisies or purple coneflowers and make a garden swag for your headboard.

Breads

Tomato & Garlic Bread

Elizabeth Ramicone
Dublin, OH

Use your bread machine during the summer months; you can enjoy the fresh taste of homemade bread without heating up the kitchen! This particular recipe is for 1-1/2 pound loaf bread machines.

1-1/4 c. warm water
2 t. oil
1/4 c. onion, finely chopped
1/3 c. dried tomatoes, thinly
    sliced
2 lg. garlic cloves, pressed

1 t. dried rosemary
3 c. bread flour
3/4 c. whole wheat flour
2 t. sugar
1 t. salt
2-1/4 t. yeast

Using the manual from your bread machine as a guide, add the ingredients in the order suggested and bake according to instructions.

Herbal Butter

Jeanne Calkins
Midland, MI

Fresh herbs make this butter so tasty!

1 green onion, finely chopped
1-1/2 t. fresh thyme, chopped
1-1/2 t. fresh basil, chopped
1-1/2 t. fresh marjoram,
    chopped

1 lb. unsalted butter, softened
2 garlic cloves, minced
juice of 1/2 a lemon

Mix onion and herbs into butter; blend in garlic and lemon juice. Allow flavors to blend 6 to 8 hours before serving. Makes one pound of herbal butter.

Peace...that was the other name for home.

-Kathleen Norris

Summertime Corn Muffins

John Alexander
New Britian, CT

Take the time to cut fresh corn from the cob for these muffins. The taste is unsurpassed and fresh corn is such a summertime treat!

3/4 c. cornmeal	1/4 c. green pepper, chopped
1/2 c. all-purpose flour	1 c. plain yogurt
2 t. baking powder	1/4 c. oil
1/2 t. baking soda	2 T. molasses
1/4 t. salt	2 T. honey
3/4 c. fresh corn kernels	1 egg, lightly beaten

Sift together first 5 ingredients; set aside. In a separate bowl, combine remaining ingredients until well blended. Combine with cornmeal mixture and stir until just blended. Lightly oil or line with paper muffin cups a 12-cup muffin pan. Spoon in batter and bake at 400 degrees for 15 minutes or until lightly golden. Makes 12 muffins.

A comfortable house is a great source of happiness.

–Sydney Smith

Breads

Lemon Balm Bread

Karen Sabrsula
Stockton, NJ

Lemon balm is a perennial herb that will reseed freely, so you'll always have an extra plant to share with a friend!

3/4 c. milk
1 c. plus 2 T. fresh lemon balm
1 T. fresh lemon thyme
1/2 c. butter, softened
1 c. sugar
2 eggs

2 c. all-purpose flour
1-1/2 t. baking powder
1/4 t. salt
zest of one lemon
1/2 c. powdered sugar
1-1/2 to 2 T. lemon juice

Combine milk, one cup lemon balm and thyme in a saucepan; gently bruise herbs to release oils. Bring to a boil then remove from heat; cover and let cool. Strain and reserve liquid; discard herbs. Cream butter and sugar; beat in eggs one at a time. In a large bowl, combine flour, baking powder and salt. Add flour mixture to butter mixture, a small amount at a time, alternating with reserved milk. Chop remaining 2 tablespoons lemon balm and add to batter; blend in lemon zest. Pour batter in a greased and floured loaf pan. Bake at 325 degrees for 45 minutes or until wooden toothpick inserted in the middle comes out clean. Cool in the pan for 10 minutes, then continue cooling on a wire rack. Combine powdered sugar and lemon juice, mix until smooth and pour over cooled bread.

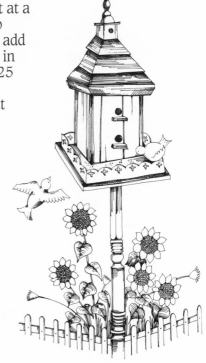

☆ *A rustic birdhouse gives your garden lots of character!*

Minted Watermelon Soup

Carol Sheets
Delaware, OH

Add sprigs of different flavored mints for variety...apple,
orange, balsam or peppermint!

1 med. watermelon, seeded and
   chopped
1-3/4 c. vanilla yogurt

Garnish: chilled watermelon
balls and sprigs of fresh mint

Place watermelon into a food processor or blender and blend until
mixture equals 6 cups. Blend with yogurt and chill 2 to 3 hours.
Spoon into custard cups or fluted glasses and garnish. Serves 6 to 8.

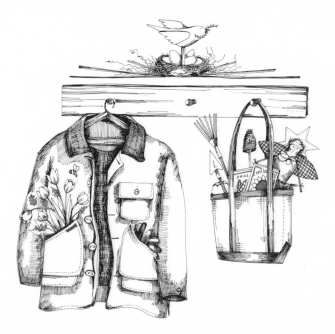

☆ *Pegboards will keep all your gardening needs close at*
hand...seed packets, gardening gloves, small tools
and gathering baskets. You'll always be able to
find just what you're looking for!

✷✷ Soups ✷✷

Golden Seafood Chowder

Joan Morris
Tallahassee, FL

I didn't think I liked oysters, so I decided to add lots of other ingredients to this soup so I could eat around them! It turns out I do like oysters and this soup has become a favorite!

1/4 lb. butter
1/4 c. onion, chopped
1 garlic clove, chopped
1 t. dried parsley
1 t. dried rosemary
1/2 t. dried thyme
1 t. dried basil
1 t. salt
6-oz. can flaked crab meat

6-1/2 oz. can chopped clams
1/2 c. white wine
1/2 c. water
1/2 lb. cod or haddock
1 c. barley
1/2 lb. shrimp
2 c. milk
1 to 2 pts. oysters

Melt butter in a 4-quart stockpot. Add onions and garlic; sauté until golden. Stir in dried herbs, salt, crab, clams, wine and water; stir well. Cut fish into bite-size pieces, blend into soup with barley; simmer 15 to 20 minutes until barley is tender and fish is cooked through. Add remaining ingredients, stir and simmer until shrimp are pink; 5 to 6 minutes.

☆ Make a portable container garden! Fill a wheelbarrow with pots of your favorite annuals...red geraniums, sunny marigolds and white alyssum are pretty. Now you can move your garden anywhere!

Basil & Tomato Soup

Vickie

*Fresh basil is unsurpassed in summer dishes;
try it in this garden-fresh soup.*

1 lg. onion, chopped	3 c. chicken broth
2 T. oil	1 c. buttermilk
2 to 3 tomatoes, chopped	1/4 c. fresh basil, minced
1-1/2 lbs. squash, chopped	Garnish: fresh basil

Sauté onion in oil over medium heat until tender. Add tomatoes and continue to cook until they become soft, about 5 minutes. Stir in squash and chicken broth; bring to boil. Reduce heat and simmer 15 minutes or until squash is fork-tender. Spoon mixture into a blender or food processor and purée with buttermilk until mixture is smooth. Sprinkle in basil; stir and garnish.

☆ *An unfinished chest or cupboard can look like an heirloom! Just stain it; let dry. Cut wallpaper to fit the lid, paste on, smooth and dry. Stain the entire chest, being careful not to brush too much on the wallpaper. When dry, seal and protect it with 3 coats of non-yellowing acrylic sealer.*

Soups

Fresh Minestrone Soup

Angela Bettencourt
Mukilteo, WA

Invite friends over for a porch supper and serve this favorite.

3 med. leeks, chopped
3 garlic cloves
3 T. olive oil
8 c. vegetable stock
15-1/2 oz. can kidney beans
1/2 t. dried basil
1/2 t. dried oregano
1/2 t. dried rosemary
salt and pepper to taste

2 c. potatoes, chopped
1 c. carrots, chopped
1/2 c. celery, chopped
1-1/2 c. squash, sliced
2 c. green beans
1/4 c. tomato paste
1/2 c. macaroni, uncooked
Garnish: fresh Parmesan cheese, grated

Cook leeks and garlic in oil for 2 to 5 minutes. Combine stock and beans with liquid, spices and vegetables; bring to a boil. Simmer for 30 minutes, then stir in tomato paste and macaroni. Cook for an additional 15 minutes. Sprinkle with Parmesan cheese. Makes 6 servings.

☆ *An old-fashioned jelly cupboard not only looks terrific, but it's great for tucking away all those little things...compact discs and cassettes, video tapes, board games, note pads and a crock filled with pens and pencils.*

Sesame Chicken Pasta Salad
Robbin Chamberlain
Worthington, OH

A really great summertime salad!

2 boneless, skinless chicken
   breasts
2 12-oz. boxes bowtie pasta
5 to 6 T. sesame seeds
3/4 c. rice vinegar
4 T. sugar
2 T. Dijon mustard
2-1/2 T. fresh ginger, grated

2 T. soy sauce
15-1/4 oz. can pineapple tidbits,
   drained, juice reserved
1/4 c. vegetable oil
2 green onions bunches, finely
   chopped
4 to 5 celery stalks, finely sliced

Place chicken breasts on hard surface, cover with plastic wrap and flatten to about 1/4 inch with rolling pin or kitchen mallet. Arrange chicken breasts in large heavy skillet; just cover with water and, uncovered, slowly bring to a simmer over low heat. When chicken begins to simmer, turn breasts, cover and remove from heat. Let sit 15 to 20 minutes or until no longer pink inside. Remove breasts to cutting board to cool. Slice into thin strips or bite-size pieces. Cook pasta according to directions; rinse under cool water. Stir sesame seeds in a heavy, dry skillet over medium heat until toasted, approximately 2 to 3 minutes. Watch closely so they don't burn; set aside. Whisk vinegar and sugar together until sugar dissolves. Add mustard, ginger and soy sauce; stir and blend in pineapple juice. Whisk well and add sesame seeds to dressing. Add oil and shake once more. Toss with chicken, pasta, pineapple, green onion and celery and refrigerate for several hours before serving.

Picnic Fruit Salad

Tina Stidam
Delaware, OH

Great for a gathering; this feeds a crowd!

3 plums, chopped
3 peaches, chopped
3 nectarines, chopped
2 c. green grapes, halved
2 c. watermelon, chopped
2 c. cantaloupe, chopped

2 c. honeydew melon, chopped
1 c. blueberries
1 c. cherries
juice of one lemon
1 c. orange juice

Mix all fruits into a large bowl. Sprinkle lemon juice and stir. Pour orange juice over the fruits and let marinate for one hour. Serves approximately 20 people.

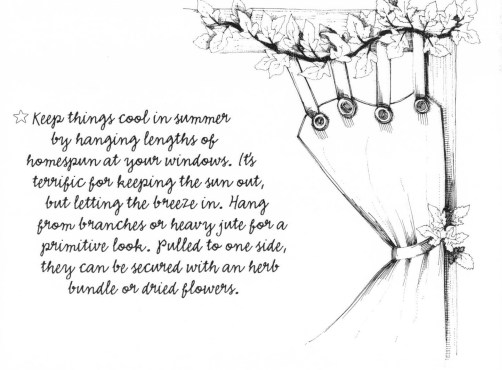

☆ Keep things cool in summer by hanging lengths of homespun at your windows. It's terrific for keeping the sun out, but letting the breeze in. Hang from branches or heavy jute for a primitive look. Pulled to one side, they can be secured with an herb bundle or dried flowers.

Shoepeg Corn Salad

Renee Johnson
Smithville, TN

I always find this is a hit at potlucks; use fresh corn if you can find it!

2 11-oz. cans white shoepeg
   corn, drained
1 med. red onion, diced
1 med. tomato, diced

1 med. cucumber, diced
1/4 c. mayonnaise-type salad
   dressing
salt and pepper to taste

Mix all ingredients together. Chill and serve.

☆ Create a cozy corner just for relaxing. Add fluffy pillows
and a pitcher of cheerful flowers. Keep a basket of
your favorite books and a garden journal close
at hand...perfect whenever you need a break!

⁂ Salads ⁑

Calico Potato Salad

Angela Murphy
Tempe, AZ

Summer is filled with activities...reunions, block parties and cookouts. This recipe is great to take along and share!

1-1/2 lbs. red potatoes, cubed
1 c. celery, sliced
2 green onions, chopped
1/4 c. red onion, sliced
1 egg, hard-boiled and chopped
1 tomato, diced
2 T. fresh dill, minced
1/2 c. mayonnaise
1 T. honey mustard

1 T. lemon juice
1 T. olive oil
1/2 to 1 T. cider vinegar
1 t. soy sauce
1 t. honey
1 t. fresh parsley, minced
1/4 t. pepper
1/4 t. celery seed

Add potatoes to a stockpot, cover with water and boil until tender. Drain and place in a serving bowl with next 6 ingredients; set aside. Blend together remaining ingredients and toss with potatoes.

Your home is where your favorite memories are.

-Pieter-Dirk Uys

BLT Salad

Carrie O'Shea
Marina Del Ray, CA

A familiar combo that might become your favorite salad!

1/4 c. buttermilk
1/4 c. mayonnaise
1/4 c. sour cream
1 T. fresh parsley, chopped
1/4 t. dried basil
1/4 t. dried oregano

1/8 t. garlic powder
8 c. lettuce, torn
1 lg. tomato, sliced
8 bacon slices, crisply cooked
   and crumbled

Blend together buttermilk, mayonnaise, sour cream, parsley, basil, oregano and garlic powder; refrigerate one to 2 hours or until chilled. Combine lettuce, tomato and bacon; toss with dressing.

☆ *Don't tuck away all those great treasures your kids found at the beach; they make great reminders of all the family fun! Shells, starfish and sand dollars can rest above a window or door, and will look beautiful layered in a cobalt blue bowl.*

Salads

Tea Room Chicken Salad

Marcia Masters
The Woodlands, TX

The addition of cashews makes this chicken salad really special!

6 c. chicken, cooked and chopped
1 pt. mayonnaise-type salad dressing
4 oz. Dijon mustard

2 c. pineapple, chopped
2 c. apple, chopped
1-1/2 t. salt
2 c. celery, thinly sliced
Garnish: 3/4 c. cashews, halved

Mix chicken with mayonnaise and mustard; blend well. Add pineapple, apple, salt and celery. Garnish with cashews before serving.

☆ *Have an annual Independence Day gathering! Bring out the noisemakers and sparklers, hang out the buntings and flags! Dress up your porch in red, white and blue! Invite neighbors over to share a glass of icy lemonade and take time to relax and visit.*

Grandma's Special Salad

Carol Shirkey
Canton, OH

Grandma always said the cherries made this salad special.

2 20-oz. cans pineapple chunks, drained
15-oz. jar maraschino cherries, drained
10-oz. can mandarin oranges, drained

8 oz. sour cream
1-1/2 c. mini-marshmallows
2 T. sugar

Blend together pineapple, cherries, oranges and sour cream. Fold in marshmallows; sprinkle with sugar. Blend and refrigerate overnight.

☆ *Stacked on shelves, folded over one another to show off their colors and patterns or framing a single block; quilts are fun to decorate with!*

Salads

My Sister's Ambrosia

Teresa Ervin
Waynesboro, VA

My sister, Donna, has been making this since she was about 10 years old. During the summer months we double or even triple it for our family gatherings!

8-oz. pkg. cream cheese,
   softened
1/3 c. sugar
2 t. lemon juice
2 t. pineapple juice
2 med. bananas, sliced and
   quartered

14-1/2 oz. jar maraschino
   cherries, halved
15-1/4 oz. can crushed
   pineapple, drained, juice
   reserved
1 c. chopped nuts
16 oz. whipped topping

Blend cream cheese, sugar and juices well. Add bananas, cherries, pineapple and nuts. Fold in whipped topping and refrigerate before serving.

☆ *Less than perfect chairs and tables found at flea markets become terrific folky furniture! Painted country colors and sponged with white paint or distressed to look old, they're a great addition to your porch!*

Pasta Nests with Vegetables

Laura Fenneman
Lima, OH

This is a great dish to fix with children when teaching them to cook. They love twirling the fettuccine and arranging the vegetables in the dish.

2 c. frozen cauliflower, broccoli
 and carrot mix
6 oz. fettuccine
3 T. butter
2 T. all-purpose flour

3/4 c. milk
1 c. sour cream
1 egg, beaten
1/4 c. grated Parmesan cheese

In separate pans, cook vegetables and pasta according to directions and drain. In saucepan, melt butter and stir in flour and milk. Cook and stir until thickened. Stir in sour cream and vegetables. Heat almost to boiling. Spoon half of mixture into a 13"x9" baking dish. Toss together cooked pasta, egg and cheese. Twirl a few strands of the fettuccine around fork and stand upright in dish to form separate nests. Spoon remaining vegetable sauce over pasta nests. Cover and bake in a 350 degree oven for 20 minutes.

☆ *Add the unexpected! Tuck recycled treasures in your flower garden...a discarded pedestal sink overflowing with impatiens, a two-tub washstand brimming with zinnias or an old iron headboard or gate for a trellis!*

✣ Sides ✣

Bountiful Green Beans

Marian Buckley
Fontana, CA

*Just-snapped beans and fresh carrots from your garden
make this recipe one your family will love.*

1/2 lb. fresh green beans,
  chopped
1 c. carrots, thinly sliced
2 green onions, chopped
1/2 c. water
1 t. sugar

1/4 t. dried thyme leaves,
  crushed
1/4 t. salt
1 t. cornstarch
1/3 c. apple juice
1/2 c. red apple, chopped

Mix together green beans, carrots, green onions, water, sugar, thyme and salt; bring to a boil. Turn heat to low and simmer, covered, until vegetables are crisp-tender; about 5 minutes. Blend cornstarch with apple juice, stirring until dissolved. Slowly stir cornstarch mixture into vegetables; add apple. Continue to simmer until sauce has thickened. Makes 6 servings.

☆ *Add a shelf above your kitchen window...it's perfect
for displaying vintage glassware from Grandma .*

Tangy Grilled Vegetables

Tiffany Brinkley
Broomfield, CO

So easy to prepare; grills in just 8 minutes!

1 t. lemon zest
1 T. fresh oregano, chopped
2 T. lemon juice
4 garlic cloves, minced
1/2 c. oil
1/4 c. white wine

1 green bell pepper, sliced
1 yellow onion, cut lengthwise
1 pt. cherry tomatoes
1 lb. red potatoes
1 lb. carrots, sliced
16 oz. mushrooms

To prepare marinade, combine lemon zest, oregano, lemon juice, garlic, oil and wine; whisk until thoroughly blended. Slide peppers, onion, tomatoes, potatoes, carrots and mushrooms on metal skewers; brush with marinade. Grill over medium-hot heat, basting with marinade, 4 minutes. Turn and grill, continuing to baste, 4 minutes longer. Serves 4.

☆ *If you have a screened-in porch or a gazebo, you have a great place to cool off from the summer sun! Fill it with white wicker furniture, plump pillows and baskets filled with your favorite books and magazines. Trumpet vine, climbing roses or grapevines can be trained to climb the walls and roof to provide even more cooling shade.*

✯ Sides ✯

Rosemary & Garlic Potatoes

Vickie

Fresh rosemary is a terrific summer herb...great with so many recipes and it adds a wonderful taste to this side dish.

1 whole garlic head
1 lb. red potatoes
1/2 lb. sm. potatoes
1 T. fresh rosemary, chopped

1 T. oil
salt and pepper to taste
Garnish: fresh rosemary sprigs

Peel the outer skin from the garlic head without peeling or separating the cloves. Place in a saucepan with potatoes, cover with water and bring to a boil. Remove from heat and drain water. In a large serving bowl, whisk together rosemary, oil, salt and pepper; toss with potatoes. Place potatoes and garlic head on a baking sheet and bake at 425 degrees for 30 minutes or until potatoes are tender. Remove from oven and separate garlic into cloves. Carefully remove skins, toss garlic cloves with potatoes, garnish with fresh rosemary.

☆ *Castoff dresser drawers make wonderful planters! Drill a few holes in the bottom, paint it a great country color and add potting soil inside. Fill with lots of your favorite flowers and enjoy!*

Settlers' Beans

Kathy Britt
Placentia, CA

You can also let this dish simmer in your slow cooker;
just set it at low for 3 to 5 hours.

1/2 lb. bacon, crisply cooked and
  crumbled, drippings reserved
1 med. onion, chopped
1 lb. ground beef, browned
15-1/2 oz. can kidney beans
15-oz. can butter beans

16-1/2 oz. can pork and beans
1/4 c. brown sugar, packed
1/2 c. barbecue sauce
1/4 c. catsup
1 t. chili powder
salt and pepper to taste

Sauté onion in 3 tablespoons reserved bacon drippings. Combine with bacon and beef; mix in beans. Add brown sugar, barbecue sauce, catsup, chili powder, salt and pepper. Spoon into a 2-quart casserole dish and bake at 350 degrees for one hour; stirring occasionally.

☆ *Give unfinished furniture an antique look with a lightly crackled finish...it's easy! Sand wood until smooth, then brush on a coat of stain; let dry. Apply a sealer and after it's dried, lightly sand. Spray on a coat of tinted crackle-finish lacquer. When the lacquer is dry, apply 2 coats of clear flat sealer to protect the finish.*

✨ Sides ✨

Tomato-Basil Torte

Cyndy Rogers
Upton, MA

*I prepare this recipe quite often in August when our garden has
an abundance of tomatoes...the aroma is irresistible!*

9-inch pie crust
1-1/2 c. mozzarella cheese,
    shredded and divided
4 med. tomatoes, thinly sliced
1/4 c. grated Parmesan cheese

2 garlic cloves, minced
1/2 c. mayonnaise
3 T. dried basil
1/8 t. pepper

Prebake pie crust in a 425 degree oven for 10 minutes; set aside to
cool slightly. Sprinkle crust with 1/2 cup of mozzarella. Arrange
tomato slices in a circular fashion on top. Mix remaining cheeses,
garlic, mayonnaise, basil and pepper together. Spread over tomatoes.
Bake at 375 degrees for 35 to 40 minutes. Makes 6 servings.

☆ *Wrapped up in embroidered handkerchiefs or floral fabrics,
make your own sachets to scent linen cupboards,
closets or drawers. Tie them to a doorknob or bedpost,
or tuck them behind your pillow!*

Jalapeño Mashed Potatoes

Rose Green
Accord, NY

If summertime isn't hot enough for you, serve these!

4 baking potatoes, peeled and
    halved
1 c. half-and-half
2 T. butter
4 jalapeño peppers, seeded and
    minced

4 scallions, sliced
salt and pepper to taste
2 T. lime zest

Place potatoes in a saucepan and cover with water. Bring to a boil and cook 15 minutes or until potatoes are tender. Combine half-and-half and butter in a small saucepan and heat until just warm. Drain potatoes and place in a bowl. Mash potatoes, slowly adding half-and-half mixture until potatoes are creamy. Stir in jalapeños, scallions, salt, pepper and lime zest.

☆ While the summer days are long, take a class to learn some of the old-fashioned crafts...make a penny or hooked rug, cross-stitch a sampler or pillow, take a spinning or weaving class.

✦ Sides ✦

Risotto with Collard Greens

Teresa Hill
Rochester, NY

This is one side dish I absolutely love!

1 sm. onion, finely chopped
1 lg. carrot, diced
2 T. olive oil
1 c. risotto, uncooked
1/2 lb. fresh collard greens,
   trimmed and torn

3 garlic cloves, minced
2 14-1/2 oz. cans chicken broth
1 c. grated Parmesan cheese
1/2 t. salt
1/2 t. pepper

Sauté onion and carrot in olive oil in a small stock pan. Add risotto and sauté until golden brown. Add collards and garlic; sauté until collards are limp. Stir in chicken broth. Cook, covered, on low heat until most of the liquid is absorbed, stirring occasionally. Add cheese, salt and pepper, blending well before serving.

☆ *Vintage advertising signs are fun and look great hanging over a mantel or doorway; look for them at yard sales or flea markets. You can also find old dairy or farm signs that would be perfect on a milk house, barn or gardening shed door!*

Hawaiian Grilled Pork Chops

Jan Stafford
Trenton, GA

*A friend brought these pork chops to a weekend camp out.
She already had them marinating, so all we did was
put them on the grill! So easy and delicious!*

20-oz. can pineapple slices,
    undrained
6 pork chops
1/2 c. soy sauce
1/3 c. vegetable oil

1/4 c. onion, minced
1 garlic clove, minced
1 T. brown sugar, packed
Garnish: pineapple rings

Drain pineapple, reserving 1/4 cup juice; set aside. Place pork chops in
a large shallow dish. Combine reserved pineapple juice, soy sauce,
vegetable oil, onion, garlic and brown sugar; mixing well. Pour over
pork chops, cover and marinate in refrigerator for at least 2 hours.
Remove pork chops, reserving marinade. Grill over medium coals for
40 to 45 minutes, turning frequently and basting with marinade.
Top each pork chop with a pineapple ring during the last 5 minutes
of grilling.

☆ *Share your favorite
flowers with all your
neighbors! Surround
your mailbox post with
climbing sweet peas,
morning glories or
scarlet runner beans.
Tall hollyhocks and bee
balm are pretty, too!*

Mains

Fajitas with Grilled Vegetables

Carol Simmons
Delaware, OH

So yummy! You can substitute your favorite vegetables if you'd like.

1-lb. boneless sirloin
3/4 c. salsa
2 T. olive oil
2 T. lime juice
2 T. tequila
2 garlic cloves, minced
1 lg. red pepper, halved
1 lg. yellow pepper, halved

4 red onion slices
1 sm. zucchini, cut lengthwise
1 sm. yellow squash, cut lengthwise
8 7-inch flour tortillas, heated
1 c. Mexican-blend cheese, shredded

Place meat in a large plastic bag. Add salsa, oil, lime juice, tequila and garlic. Close bag securely; turn to combine all ingredients and to coat the meat. Add vegetables and coat. Marinate in refrigerator at least 2 hours. Remove meat and vegetables from marinade. Grill beef and vegetables 4 to 5 inches from heat for about 5 minutes per side or until beef is medium-rare. Remove to carving board; slice beef and peppers into thin strips, squash into slices and separate onion into rings. To serve, divide beef and vegetables among tortillas. Heat remaining marinade to a boil and drizzle over beef and vegetables. Sprinkle with cheese; roll and serve with marinade on the side.

Until you have heard the whippoorwill, either nearby or in the faint distance, you have not experienced a summer night.

-Henry Beetle Hough

Summertime Shish-Kabobs

Tina Stidam
Delaware, OH

Try beef, chicken or seafood...all are great!

2 c. oil
1/2 c. vinegar
1 T. soy sauce
1 t. ginger
2 t. garlic, pressed
2 t. dried dill weed

1-1/2 to 2 lb. sirloin beef, sliced
4 potatoes, boiled and chopped
12 cherry tomatoes
1 green pepper, sliced
1 onion, sliced

In medium bowl, mix oil, vinegar, soy sauce, ginger, garlic and dill weed. Place beef in marinade for 8 to 16 hours, stirring occasionally. Alternate meat and vegetables on wooden skewers. Cook over charcoal or under a broiler for 10 minutes or until meat is to desired doneness. Makes 6 to 8 servings.

☆ *Punch holes in the bottom of mismatched cookware, coffee pots and tea kettles, fill with dirt and add your favorite flowers. Line them up side-by-side on a weathered country bench!*

Lemon & Garlic Chicken

Kathleen Richter
Bridgeport, CT

The chicken is so tender it falls off the bone!

3 to 5-lb. roasting chicken
1 lemon, halved

7 whole garlic cloves
salt and pepper to taste

Rinse chicken and pat dry. Place both halves of lemon inside chicken. Take 3 cloves of garlic and place between the skin and the meat. Place 4 garlic cloves in the cavity along with the lemons. Season entire chicken with salt and pepper. Bake for one hour and 40 minutes at 350 degrees, or until a meat thermometer registers 170 degrees in the breast and 185 degrees in the thigh Let sit 10 minutes before carving.

Green Enchilada Casserole

Corrine Lane
Gooseberry Patch

A great summertime dish topped with fresh homemade salsa!

15-oz. bag white tortilla chips,
  crushed
1-1/2 lbs. ground beef
1 sm. onion, chopped
salt and pepper to taste
garlic salt to taste
4-oz. can chopped green chilies
1 to 2 jalapeños, chopped

1/2 c. picante sauce
10-3/4 oz. can cream of
  mushroom soup
1/2 c. water
1/2 c. sour cream
2-1/2 c. Cheddar or Monterey
  Jack cheese, shredded

Cover the bottom of a 13"x9" glass baking dish with tortilla chips. Brown beef; add onions and sauté. Season with salt, pepper and garlic salt; add chilies, jalapeños, picante sauce, soup and water. Simmer until soup is well blended; stir in sour cream. Pour half the meat mixture over the tortilla chips, top with half the cheese; repeat. Bake at 350 degrees for 25 to 30 minutes.

Sweet-Hot Ribeye Steaks

Erin Doell
Glen Ellyn, IL

Juicy and tender, perfect with some roasted sweet corn!

2 garlic cloves, crushed
2 t. water
2 T. sweet-hot mustard
1 t. fresh rosemary, chopped

salt and pepper to taste
1/2 t. fresh thyme, chopped
2 1-lb. ribeye steaks

In a microwave-safe dish, combine garlic and water. Microwave on high 30 seconds. Blend in sweet-hot mustard, rosemary, salt, pepper and thyme; stir well. Brush sweet-hot mustard sauce on both sides of steaks and grill over coals 12 minutes for medium, adjusting grilling time for desired doneness.

Country-Style BBQ Sauce

Tami Bowman
Gooseberry Patch

Great for summertime grilling! Use on chicken or ribs.

1/2 c. onion, chopped
1 T. oil
1 c. catsup
3/4 c. water

1/3 c. vinegar
1/2 c. brown sugar, packed
1 t. Worcestershire sauce
1/4 t. celery seed

Sauté onion in oil until tender; blend in catsup, water, vinegar, brown sugar, Worcestershire sauce and celery seed. Let mixture simmer for 20 minutes or until sauce thickens.

Great-American Submarine

Jo Ann

Great for summertime get-togethers!

16-oz. loaf Italian bread
1/2 c. mayonnaise
1/2 lb. honey ham, thinly sliced
1/2 lb. salami, thinly sliced
1 lg. tomato, thinly sliced
1 c. onion, thinly sliced
1 lg. green pepper, thinly sliced

1/2 lb. Muenster cheese, sliced
2 3.8-oz. cans sliced black
  olives
2 banana peppers, seeded and
  sliced
1 bunch red leaf lettuce, torn
salt and pepper to taste

Cut bread loaf in half horizontally; spread mayonnaise over bottom half of bread. Layer remaining ingredients in order, top with remaining half of bread. Slice and serve.

☆ *Childhood toys add a feel of nostalgia wherever you set them. Sailboats or airplanes, Teddy bears or tea sets all bring back fond memories. Set them on tables, stairs, cupboard shelves or mantels.*

Barbecue Beef

Laura Strausberger
Roswell, GA

This recipe came from my mother, Lois, the greatest cook I know. She would make this recipe for parties, picnics, church events and for our family. It smells wonderful simmering on the stove and there are never any leftovers!

2-1/2 lbs. pot roast, cooked and
    shredded
2 c. catsup
1 green pepper, chopped
2 onions, chopped
1 T. sugar

2 t. dry mustard
2 t. vinegar
1/2 t. cinnamon
1 t. salt
1/4 t. cloves

To shredded roast, add catsup, green pepper, onions, sugar, dry mustard, vinegar, cinnamon, salt and cloves. Simmer for one hour or until mixture thickens to desired consistency. Serve on warm buns.

Home is a place you grow up wanting to leave, and grow old wanting to come back to.

-John Ed Pearce

Mains

Garlic & Mustard Burgers

Delores Begansky
West Willington, CT

Who doesn't like hamburgers on the grill?
Try this recipe for your next cook out!

1 lb. ground beef
3 T. country-style Dijon mustard
5 garlic cloves, chopped
4 hamburger buns

4 Monterey Jack cheese slices
14-oz. jar roasted bell peppers, drained

Heat coals on grill. Mix beef, mustard and garlic together. Shape into 4 patties about 3/4-inch thick. Cover and grill patties for 12 to 15 minutes. Top burgers with cheese and roasted bell peppers.

☆ Decorate walls, floors and furniture with stencils! On floors create a border around the edges or make a "rug" in the middle of the room. Add a stenciled chair rail, ceiling border, swags at window corners or a cheerful greeting above your door. Add leaves, berries or flower designs to your kitchen cupboards and tabletops or even stencil a wreath on your front door!

Elephant Ears

Phyllis Peters
Three Rivers, MI

Don't wait for the county fair to enjoy an elephant ear, prepare them yourself for family and friends and share this delicious treat!

1 pkg. active yeast
1 c. warm water
2 eggs, beaten
6 T. sugar, divided

4 c. all-purpose flour
vegetable oil
1 t. cinnamon

Soften yeast in water, cool. Combine yeast mixture with eggs, 3 tablespoons sugar and flour; blend well. Divide dough into 12 pieces and let rest 20 minutes. Roll each piece of dough in a large circle on lightly floured surface; stretch with your hands if needed. Heat one inch of vegetable oil in large iron skillet, and cook each circle until lightly browned, turn once, surface will bubble. Remove and place on paper towels. Combine remaining sugar and cinnamon; sprinkle over each circle.

☆ *This is the year to build a tree house for the kids! They'll love having a place to dream and call their own. Stock it with binoculars, books, maps, paper, pencils and sleeping bags!*

Strawberry Shortcake

Lisa Watkins
Gooseberry Patch

One of the best things about summer...strawberries!

3 c. strawberries, washed and
   sliced
6 T. sugar, divided
1-1/2 c. all-purpose flour
2 t. baking powder

1 t. salt
6 T. butter, divided
3/4 c. milk
Garnish: whipped cream

Combine strawberries and 5 tablespoons sugar; set aside for 30 minutes. Combine flour, baking powder, salt and remaining tablespoon of sugar. Cut 4 tablespoons butter into flour mixture using a pastry cutter or 2 knives, until mixture resembles crumbs; blend in milk. On a lightly floured surface, roll dough 2 inches thick and approximately 6 inches long. Place dough on an ungreased cookie sheet and bake at 400 degrees for 12 to 15 minutes; until golden. Remove from oven, cool slightly and slice in half horizontally. Spread remaining butter on cut sides. To serve, spoon strawberries over bottom half of shortcake, top with remaining half and spoon additional strawberries on top. Serve with whipped cream if desired.

Roses are red,
violets are blue,
honey is sweet
and so are you!

-Anonymous

Old-Fashioned Jam Cake

Jan Marler
Crestview, FL

This is my grandmother's old-fashioned recipe.

1 c. buttermilk
1 t. baking soda
1 t. baking powder
1/2 c. boiling water
2 eggs, beaten
4-1/2 c. sugar, divided
2/3 c. plus 4 T. shortening,
    divided
1 c. raisins
1 c. blackberry jam

1 c. applesauce
1 c. pecans, chopped
3 c. all-purpose flour
1/2 c. cocoa
1 t. cinnamon
1 t. allspice
1 t. nutmeg
4 T. butter
1 c. milk
1 t. vanilla extract

In a large bowl, blend together buttermilk, baking soda, baking powder and boiling water. In a separate bowl, cream together eggs, 2 cups sugar and 2/3 cup shortening. Combine buttermilk mixture and egg mixture; fold in raisins, jam, applesauce and pecans; mixing well. Stir in flour, cocoa, cinnamon, allspice and nutmeg. Lightly oil and flour 3 round 9" cake pans and divide batter among all 3 pans. Bake at 350 degrees for 30 to 35 minutes or until cakes test done; cool. Prepare icing by combining remaining shortening, butter, milk and 2 cups sugar in a saucepan; bring to a boil. In medium saucepan, brown 1/2 cup sugar, stirring constantly to avoid burning. Add browned sugar to shortening mixture and stir in vanilla. Ice cake and serve.

Desserts

Luscious Lemonade Pie

Danielle Graves
Wichita, KS

This is a wonderfully refreshing treat to serve all summer long!

6-oz. can frozen lemonade
14-oz. can sweetened condensed
   milk

2 drops yellow food coloring
8 oz. whipped topping
9-inch graham cracker pie crust

Mix together lemonade and milk. If desired, add food coloring for a lemony color. Fold in whipped topping, and pour into the crust. Refrigerate a few hours or overnight.

☆ Colorful depression-era glassware is so pretty to collect. You can find lots of pastel colors; pink, blue, green or yellow and designs with nostalgic names like iris, cabbage rose, meadow wreath, cherry blossom or buttons & bows.

Strawberry Ice Cream

Diane Focken
Ansley, NE

The best on a hot day! Let the kids take turns turning the crank if you have an old-fashioned ice-cream maker!

2 3-oz. pkgs. strawberry gelatin
1-1/2 c. boiling water
2 c. sugar
4 eggs
3 c. cream

2 t. vanilla extract
1/8 t. salt
2 10-oz. pkgs. frozen
  strawberries, thawed
milk

Dissolve gelatin in boiling water. Stir in sugar and mix until dissolved. Stir in eggs, cream, vanilla and salt; mix well. Stir in strawberries, pour into ice cream freezer and add enough milk to fill to line. Freeze according to manufacturer's instructions or hand crank until ice cream hardens.

Lemon Lush

Crystal Gwynn
Parkersburg, WV

This is a favorite at our house...from kids to adults!

1 c. all-purpose flour
1/2 c. butter, melted
1/2 c. pecan pieces
8-oz. pkg. cream cheese
1 c. sugar

2 c. whipped topping, divided
3 3-1/2 oz. pkgs. instant lemon
  pudding,
4-1/2 c. milk

Combine flour, butter and pecan pieces. Press mixture into the bottom of a 13"x9" pan. Bake at 375 degrees for 12 to 15 minutes. Mix together cream cheese, sugar and one cup whipped topping. Spoon on crust while still warm, not hot, and smooth out evenly. Combine pudding mixes and milk; beat for 2 minutes. Pour over the cooled crust mixture. Top with remaining whipped topping.

Desserts

Independence Day Dessert
Jo Ann

A pretty dessert for your summer picnics!

10-oz. pkg. frozen puff pastry
   shells
1/2 c. seedless raspberry jam
1 t. lemon juice
1 c. strawberries, sliced

1 c. blueberries
1 c. raspberries
Garnish: vanilla yogurt or
   whipped cream

Bake pastry shells according to package directions; set aside. Place raspberry jam in a small pan and melt over low heat; stirring constantly. When melted, remove from heat and blend in lemon juice and berries. Spoon into pastry shells and top with yogurt or whipped cream.

☆ *Summer is the perfect time to show off your creative talents! During the months your fireplace isn't in use, stencil or paint 3 boards in nautical or patriotic themes, attach hinges and you've created a summertime fireplace screen!*

✦⋆ Summer ⋆✦

☆ **Host a family reunion** this summer! Drape tables with red, white and blue quilts or red checked tablecloths, fill sap buckets with wildflowers and toss lots of cozy pillows on the porch swing!

☆ **Put a lady scarecrow** in your garden! Start with a simple cross-shaped scarecrow, slip on a long-sleeved dress and then an apron. Place an upside-down watering can on for her head and dress her up with a wide-brimmed straw hat!

☆ **Nothing brightens a picnic table more** than sunflowers! Tuck them into an old tea kettle or watering can; you'll have an instant centerpiece.

☆ **A country-style ice bucket**…find a bucket that just fits inside the top of an open milk can. Fill the bucket with ice, add a bottle of sparkling grape juice and slip the bucket inside the milk can.

☆ Summer ☆

☆ **Vintage pop bottle crates** make terrific garden totes. Seed packets, small tools and gardening gloves will easily fit inside!

☆ **Whitewashed 6-pane window frames** can easily become a gardener's bulletin board! Tap a sawtooth hanger on the back, criss-cross the frame with jute and hang on the wall. Tuck in seed packets, a wish-list of flowers, gardening tips and photographs of gardens for ideas and inspiration...everything will be at your fingertips.

☆ **Rain barrels** are great for holding your tall garden tools...rakes, hoes, spades, weeders or shovels fit nicely inside!

☆ **Discarded oval picture frames** make a whimsical chalkboard to let visitors know you're in the garden! Cut a lightweight piece of wood to fit the opening, spray with chalkboard paint; let dry, then nail to the back of the frame opening.

Turkey Pinwheels

Pat Habiger
Spearville, KS

A yummy appetizer for a tailgate party!

1/4 c. celery, finely chopped
2 T. onion, finely chopped
2 T. butter
2 c. turkey, cooked and finely
   chopped
1/4 t. poultry seasoning

1-1/4 c. all-purpose flour
2 t. baking powder
1/2 t. salt
1/4 c. shortening
1/2 c. milk

Cook celery and onion in butter until tender. Add turkey and poultry seasoning; mix. Preheat oven to 450 degrees; grease baking sheet. Stir flour, baking powder and salt together. Mix in shortening until mixture resembles coarse cornmeal. Add milk; mix just enough to moisten dry ingredients. Turn dough onto lightly floured surface. Roll into a 10"x6" rectangle. Spread turkey mixture evenly over dough. Roll up jelly-roll style. Cut into 6 slices. Place slices on baking sheet; bake 20 to 25 minutes or until lightly browned.

Fill autumn windowboxes with straw, gourds, mini pumpkins and Indian corn!

Appetizers

Hayride Popcorn & Peanuts

Shelley Turner
Boise, ID

A quick snack you can take along for munching!

1/3 c. butter, melted
1 t. dried dill weed
1 t. Worcestershire sauce
1/2 t. garlic powder
1/2 t. onion powder

1/4 t. salt
2 qts. popcorn, popped
2 1-1/2 oz. cans potato sticks
1 c. mixed nuts

In a large mixing bowl, blend first 6 ingredients together well. Add popcorn, potato sticks and nuts. Toss mixture and place on an ungreased baking sheet. Bake at 350 degrees for 3 minutes, stir mixture and bake another 4 to 5 minutes.

Bowl Game Dip

Judy Kelly
St. Charles, MO

All the men love this!

4 oz. hot sausage
1 sm. onion, chopped
4-1/2 oz. can chopped green
　chilies

14-1/2 oz. can tomatoes
8 oz. sour cream
8-oz. pkg. cream cheese

Fry sausage and onion in skillet together until sausage is thoroughly cooked; drain grease. Add green chilies and tomatoes and cook, uncovered, for 15 minutes. Add sour cream and cream cheese. Simmer for 30 minutes, stirring often. Keep warm when serving with chips or crackers.

Nuts, ripe brown, come showering down in the bountiful days of September!

– Mary Howitt

Sweet & Sassy Meatballs

Phyllis Dill
Columbus, NJ

An excellent appetizer; it's different from other recipes!

1/2 c. bread crumbs
1 egg
2 T. onion, minced
2 T. fresh parsley, minced
1 t. salt

1/2 t. pepper
2 lbs. ground sirloin
1/2 c. catsup
12-oz. jar apple jelly

Mix bread crumbs, egg, onion, parsley, salt and pepper together. Add to meat and blend thoroughly. In a large pot, mix catsup and apple jelly; bring mixture to a boil and stir to blend together. Form meat into one-inch balls and drop into boiling mixture. Reduce heat and simmer slowly, for 30 minutes.

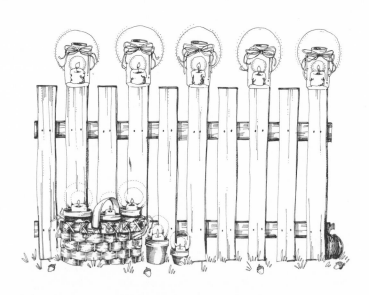

Light the way for little trick-or-treaters with tea lights tucked in mason jars, terra cotta pots or hollowed out mini pumpkins.

Appetizers

Acorn Squash Spread

Christina Nancarrow
Northwood, NH

Serve this dip with squares of cranberry or date nut bread.

1 acorn squash, top cut off   8-oz. pkg. cream cheese

Bake squash at 350 degrees for 30 to 45 minutes, or until done. Remove from oven and let cool slightly. Scrape out seeds and discard. Carefully scrape out squash, leaving skin of squash intact. Mix squash with cream cheese. Pour mixture back into squash shell. Serve chilled or at room temperature.

Heavenly Sliced Apple Dip

Karen Ray
Mission Viejo, CA

After we go apple picking in the fall, we come home to make this quick and tasty treat!

2 3-oz. pkgs. cream cheese,   1-1/2 t. vanilla extract
   softened   1/2 c. chopped pecans
3/4 c. brown sugar, packed   6 c. green apples, sliced
1/4 c. sugar   lemon juice

Mix cream cheese, sugars, vanilla and pecans together; chill. Toss apples with enough lemon juice to coat. Serve with dip.

🌰 *Wrap a length of wire around the neck of a canning jar and secure tightly. Add some sand and a votive inside then hang them from tree branches or fence posts!*

Spiced Hot Cider

Sally Borland
Port Gibson, NY

*After raking leaves or taking a long walk on a cool day, it's fun
to gather as a family over a hot cup of cider.*

1 gal. cider
1 c. brown sugar, packed
6-oz. can frozen orange juice

1 cinnamon stick
3 whole cloves
3 whole allspice

Heat all ingredients and simmer. Remove spices before serving;
serves 10.

Pumpkin Dip

Missy Backues
Jefferson City, MO

Great served with apple slices, gingersnaps or vanilla wafers.

2 8-oz. pkgs. cream cheese,
    softened
15-oz. can pumpkin
1/2 t. pumpkin pie spice

1/4 t. nutmeg
1/2 t. cinnamon
1 lb. powdered sugar

Blend cream cheese with mixer until smooth. Add pumpkin and spices
to cream cheese mixture; fold in powdered sugar. Chill before serving.

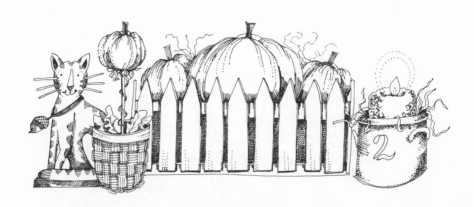

Appetizers

Harvest Zucchini Squares
Jo Ann

All that zucchini in your garden makes more than zucchini bread...try these tasty appetizer squares!

3 zucchini, shredded
1 c. biscuit baking mix
1/2 c. onion, chopped
1/2 c. grated Parmesan cheese
2 T. fresh parsley, chopped

1/2 t. dried oregano
salt and pepper to taste
1 garlic clove, minced
1/2 c. vegetable oil
4 eggs, slightly beaten

Blend all ingredients together and pour into an oiled 13"x9" baking dish. Bake at 350 degrees for 25 minutes. Cool slightly and cut into squares.

Hot Apple Drink
Tammy Dycus
Gainesboro, TN

Serve in tall mugs with a cinnamon stick!

1/2 gal. apple juice
1 t. whole allspice
1 qt. cranberry juice cocktail
3/4 c. brown sugar, packed

2 c. water
2 cinnamon sticks, broken
1 t. whole cloves

Combine all ingredients in a 5-quart Dutch oven. Place spices in a tea strainer. Simmer on low for 2 hours; remove spices and serve.

Decorate birdhouses with bunches of bittersweet and clusters of Indian corn!

Pumpkin Coffeecake

Gail Hageman
Albion, ME

*A co-worker shared this recipe with me and
it's been a hit at every potluck!*

2 16-oz. boxes pound cake mix
4 t. pumpkin pie spice
2 t. baking soda
3/4 c. water
15-oz. can pumpkin

4 eggs
3/4 c. brown sugar, packed
3/4 c. walnuts, chopped
1/2 c. all-purpose flour
1/3 c. cold butter

Mix cake mix, pumpkin pie spice and baking soda together. Blend in water, pumpkin and eggs. Beat until well mixed. Pour half the batter into a greased 13"x9" pan. To prepare crumb streusel, blend together remaining ingredients in a small bowl until crumbly. Sprinkle half of the crumb streusel on top of batter. Pour remaining batter into pan. Sprinkle remaining crumb topping on top. Bake at 325 degrees for 50 minutes.

*The true essentials of
a feast are only fun
and feed.*

—Holmes

Blue Ribbon Molasses Bread

Marilyn Behe
Little Falls, NY

My grandmother's molasses bread is a family favorite;
especially topped with melted butter!

1 c. boiling water
1 c. sugar
2 eggs
1/2 c. molasses

1/2 c. oil
2 c. all-purpose flour
2 t. baking soda
1 t. salt

Mix boiling water and remaining ingredients until well blended. Pour into an oiled 9"x5" loaf pan. Bake at 350 degrees for approximately one hour.

Pecan Pie Muffins

Dora Poythress
Lawrenceville, VA

Moist and delicious! I doubled the recipe the last time I
made them and there were only a few left over!

1 c. brown sugar, packed
1/2 c. all-purpose flour
1 c. pecans, chopped

2/3 c. butter, melted
2 eggs, beaten

Combine brown sugar, flour and pecans and set aside. Combine butter and eggs; mix well. Stir into flour mixture until moistened. Fill paper-lined miniature muffin cups, 2/3 full. Bake at 350 degrees for 20 to 25 minutes or until they test done. Remove and cool on racks. Makes 2-1/2 dozen mini muffins.

Popovers

Kara Allison
Dublin, OH

Mom's beef stew wasn't complete without a batch of popovers straight from the oven. As kids we'd peel the tops off and use them to sop up the leftover stew in the bottom of our bowls. We'd butter the bottoms and eat them while the steam was still escaping.

1 c. milk	1/4 t. salt
1 T. butter, melted	2 eggs
1 c. all-purpose flour	

All ingredients should be at room temperature before beginning. Beat milk, butter, flour and salt together. Blend in eggs, one at time, being sure not to over beat. Fill buttered, large muffin pans 3/4 full; don't overfill. Bake at once in a 450 degree oven for 15 minutes, then lower the heat to 350 degrees and bake about 20 minutes longer. To test doneness, remove a popover to be sure the side walls are firm. If not cooked long enough, the popover will collapse. You may want to insert a sharp paring knife gently into the other popovers to allow the steam to escape after baking.

Fill urns with straw and set a big pumpkin in the middle...a cheery autumn welcome!

Breads

Apple Bread

Kathy Grashoff
Ft. Wayne, IN

Share a loaf with a friend!

4 eggs
2 c. sugar
1 c. vegetable oil
1 t. salt

1 t. vanilla extract
1 t. baking soda
3 c. all-purpose flour
3 c. apples, sliced

Preheat oven to 300 degrees. Combine all ingredients and mix with an electric mixer. Pour batter into 2 greased and floured 9"x5" loaf pans. Bake for 1-1/2 hours. Makes 2 loaves.

Classic Cornbread

Tami Bowman
Gooseberry Patch

There's nothing better with a bowl of chili or stew!

1 c. all-purpose flour
4 t. baking powder
1 t. salt
1/4 c. sugar

1 c. milk
1/4 c. oil
1 c. yellow cornmeal
2 eggs

Preheat oven to 400 degrees. Grease the bottom of an 8" square baking pan. Sift together flour, baking powder, salt and sugar. In a medium-size mixing bowl, mix milk, oil and cornmeal; adding flour mixture gradually. Add eggs and mix until batter is smooth. Pour into pan and bake for 25 to 30 minutes. Serve hot.

Dorothy's Yeast Rolls

Phyllis Peters
Three Rivers, MI

*This recipe was shared with me 45 years ago
and still remains my favorite.*

2 pkgs. active yeast
2 c. warm water
1/2 c. sugar
3 T. margarine

7 c. all-purpose flour
1 egg, beaten
1 t. salt

Soften yeast in water; set aside. Combine remaining ingredients, add yeast mixture and blend well. Knead on lightly floured board, place in bowl and cover with damp cloth. Let rise until double in bulk; about 2 hours. Punch down, form into balls and place close together in 2 oiled 9" round pans, cover, let rise. Bake at 375 degrees for 10 to 12 minutes or until done and lightly golden. Makes approximately 2 dozen rolls.

Use baskets, pottery, Shaker boxes, crocks or sugar buckets for beautiful fall table arrangements. Fill them with mini pumpkins, apples, gourds, nuts, artichokes and colorful leaves.

Breads

Oatmeal-Honey Bread

Robyn Wright
Delaware, OH

A hearty bread! Great for sandwiches or alongside a bowl of soup.

1 c. rolled oats
2-1/4 c. water, divided
1 T. active dry yeast
1/3 c. honey

2 t. salt
1 T. butter
5-1/2 c. all-purpose flour

Place oats into a large bowl. Bring 2 cups of water to a boil and pour over the oats; let stand at least 15 minutes. Stir the yeast into 1/4 cup warm water and let stand 5 minutes. Feel the oats at the bottom of the bowl to make sure they are lukewarm, not hot. When oats are lukewarm, add honey, salt, butter and dissolved yeast. Work in flour 1/2 cup at a time until dough is smooth and elastic, adding more flour as needed. Place dough in a greased bowl, turning to coat dough. Cover with a clean cloth and let rise in a barely warmed oven for about 40 to 50 minutes or until doubled in bulk. Punch down dough, shape into 2 loaves and place in greased 9"x5" loaf pans and let rise until doubled. Bake at 350 degrees for 35 to 40 minutes. Cool on racks.

Here's to October...
frost-kissed apples; the
wild-as-the-wind smell of
hickory nuts and the
nostalgic whiff of that
first wood smoke.

-Ken Weber

Buttermilk Rolls

Rhonda Reeder
Ellicott City, MD

Top with real butter and enjoy warm from the oven...the best!

1 pkg. active yeast
1 c. warm buttermilk
3 T. shortening, melted
1 t. brown sugar, packed

1/4 t. baking soda
2-1/4 c. wheat flour
1 t. baking powder
1-1/4 t. salt

Dissolve yeast in buttermilk; blend in shortening, brown sugar and baking soda. Combine wheat flour, baking powder and salt; add to buttermilk mixture. Stir one minute, cover and let rise until double in bulk. Punch down and let rise again until double. Knead on a lightly floured board for 10 minutes. Roll into one-inch balls and place 3 balls in each cup of buttered muffin tins; cover with a damp cloth. Let dough rise again until desired height. Bake at 425 degrees for 15 to 20 minutes, or until golden.

Fall is the perfect time for flea markets and auctions! Dress comfortably and take along extra blankets and rope so you can safely and easily take your new finds home!

Apple-Cinnamon Rolls

Tori Willis
Champaign, IL

Wonderful for a cool autumn morning with a glass of icy milk!

6 to 6-1/2 c. all-purpose flour, divided
2 pkgs. instant dry yeast
2 c. milk
1/4 c. sugar
3/4 c. margarine, melted and divided
1-1/2 t. salt
1 egg
1 c. brown sugar, packed
2 t. plus 1/4 t. cinnamon, divided
3/4 c. apple butter
2 c. apples, peeled and chopped
1 c. powdered sugar
1 to 3 T. apple juice

Combine 3 cups of the flour and yeast; set aside. In a saucepan, mix milk, sugar, 1/4 cup margarine and salt until warm and margarine begins to melt; stir into flour mixture. Add egg and beat on low for one minute. Increase speed to high for 3 minutes. Blend as much of the remaining flour as you can with a spoon. On a lightly floured surface, knead in enough of the remaining flour until dough is smooth. Place dough in an oiled bowl, turning to coat all sides. Let rise in a warm place for one hour or until double in bulk. Mix brown sugar, remaining margarine and 2 teaspoons cinnamon; stir in apple butter and apple; set aside. When dough has risen, punch down and place on a lightly floured surface. Divide dough in half and let rest 10 minutes. Roll each section of dough into a 16"x12" rectangle and top with half of the apple filling. Roll up each half of dough, jelly-roll style, beginning with the short end. Cut each roll into 6 slices and place, cut side down on a greased 13"x9" pan. Let rise until double then bake at 350 degrees for 35 to 40 minutes. Let cool for 10 minutes. Blend together powdered sugar, remaining cinnamon and one tablespoon apple juice; add more apple juice, one teaspoon at a time until icing is desired consistency. Drizzle over rolls. Makes 12.

Autumn is a second spring when every leaf is a flower.

-Albert Camus

Country Vegetable Soup

Carol Shirkey
Canton, OH

Our family loves this in cold weather and it's so easy to prepare!

2 lbs. stew beef
2 lg. potatoes, diced
2 onions, chopped
3 carrots, sliced
2 celery stalks, sliced
6 to 8 parsley sprigs
1 T. salt

1/2 t. thyme
1/4 t. pepper
1-lb. can chopped tomatoes,
    undrained
16-oz. pkg. frozen mixed
    vegetables, thawed

Combine all ingredients, except mixed vegetables in a 4-quart slow cooker; fill tomato can with water and stir into soup. Cook on low for 10 to 11 hours. Add mixed vegetables and continue to cook until heated through. Makes 6 to 8 servings.

Football Stew

Lorna Manny
North Dartmouth, MA

Just put it in the oven and forget about it!

2 lbs. stew beef
4 potatoes, chopped
6 carrots, sliced
3 to 4 onions, chopped
1 c. celery, chopped

15-1/4 oz. can peas
16-oz. can tomatoes
1 bread slice, cubed
salt and pepper to taste

Do not brown meat. Combine all ingredients in a 2-quart casserole dish. Cover with foil and bake at 250 degrees for 5 hours. Serves 6.

Soups

Hearty Ham & Bean Soup

*Kathleen Westby
Lansing, MI*

I keep a mix of dried beans on hand to use for soup and to give as gifts. Just put the beans in a jar and tie on the recipe!

1/4 c. barley
1/4 c. dried black beans
1/4 c. dried red beans
1/4 c. dried pinto beans
1/4 c. dried navy beans
1/4 c. dried black-eyed beans
1/4 c. dried Great Northern
  beans
1/4 c. dried lentils

1/4 c. dried split peas
2 qts. water
1-lb. ham, cooked and diced
1 lg. onion, chopped
1 garlic clove, minced
1/2 to 3/4 t. salt
16-oz. can tomatoes, undrained
10-oz. can tomatoes and green
  chilies, undrained

Sort and wash beans and place in Dutch oven. Cover with water, 2 inches above beans; let soak overnight. Drain beans. Add 2 quarts fresh water, ham, onion, garlic and salt. Cover and bring to a boil. Reduce heat and simmer 1-1/2 hours or until beans are tender. Add remaining ingredients; simmer 30 minutes, stirring occasionally.

Almost anything gathered from your yard or garden can become a colorful autumn centerpiece. Top a farm table with leaves, apples, pumpkins, acorns, bittersweet and sunflower heads.

Butternut Squash Soup

Audrey Lett
Newark, DE

A creamy soup that's great for an autumn picnic. Bike to a quiet spot, spread out a blanket and enjoy the fall colors.

2 lg. butternut squash, halved and seeded
1/4 c. oil
2 lbs. carrots, peeled and chopped
3 Granny Smith apples, peeled and chopped

1 lg. onion, finely chopped
3 green onions, minced
2 T. garlic, minced
8 c. water
salt and pepper to taste
2 c. heavy whipping cream

In a 350 degree oven, bake squash, skin side down, until squash is tender, about 30 minutes. Spoon out squash; set aside. Combine oil, carrots, apples, onion, green onions and garlic; sauté for 2 minutes. Stir in squash and water. Bring to a boil then reduce heat and simmer 45 minutes; stir in salt and pepper to taste. Carefully pour soup, a little at a time, into a blender and purée until smooth. Add back to saucepan and blend in cream. Serves 6.

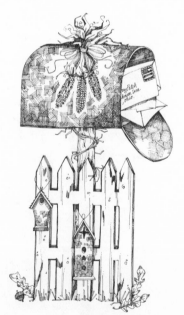

An autumn welcome...a basket of gourds and pumpkins by the mailbox and corn shocks tied around the post. Bunches of Indian corn can be draped on either side and topped with raffia bows!

Soups

Vermont Potato Soup

Coli Harrington
Delaware, OH

When I lived in Vermont the winters were so cold; this soup is one that would warm us right up!

1 c. onions, chopped
1 garlic clove, minced
3 T. butter
4 c. chicken broth
4 lg. potatoes, cubed
2 T. fresh parsley, chopped

salt and pepper to taste
2 c. Cheddar cheese, grated
Garnish: 4 bacon slices, crisply
　cooked and crumbled and
　3/4 c. croutons, crushed

Combine onions, garlic and butter in a Dutch oven and cook for 5 minutes. Blend in chicken broth, potatoes, parsley, salt and pepper to taste. Simmer, covered, for 20 minutes then remove from heat. Spoon mixture in a food processor and purée small amounts at a time. Place soup back in Dutch oven and stir in Cheddar cheese; heat through. Combine bacon and croutons; sprinkle over soup before serving. Makes 6 servings.

Invite friends and neighbors to a harvest supper! Set up tables outside covered with colorful camp blankets, centerpieces of potted mums, and lots of glowing Jack-o'-lanterns.

Harvest Squash & Mushroom Soup

Cheri Maxwell
Gulf Breeze, FL

*Fresh squash is easily available this time of year, why
not try this tasty soup to warm you right up!*

3 c. butternut squash
1/2 c. onion, diced
2 garlic cloves, crushed
1-1/4 t. salt
1/2 t. cumin
1/2 t. coriander
1/2 t. cinnamon

3/4 t. ginger
1/4 t. dry mustard
1/8 t. cayenne pepper
2 T. butter, melted
8 oz. mushrooms, sliced
2-1/2 c. chicken broth

Slice squash in half, seed and place in an oven-safe pan filled with
water. Bake at 375 degrees for 30 minutes or until tender. Let cool
until easy to handle and chop, measuring out 3 cups. Combine onion,
garlic, salt and spices in butter and sauté until tender. Stir in
mushrooms and cook 10 minutes longer. In a blender, combine
squash, chicken broth and onion mixture and purée. Return to a
saucepan to heat through before serving.

Soups

Mother's Pasta Fagioli

Jane Patterson
Durham, CT

We all have childhood memories that give us pleasure. To me, this recipe brings back the memory of my mother in the kitchen preparing dinner. Her cooking would always fill us with a feeling of well-being.

15-1/2 oz. can red kidney beans
15-1/2 oz. can white kidney beans
15-1/2 oz. can garbanzo beans
1/4 c. olive oil
2 T. garlic, minced
1 sm. onion, finely chopped
2 celery stalks, chopped
1 carrot, chopped
1 med. potato, finely diced

14-1/2 oz. can Italian tomatoes, chopped, reserving juice
2 c. water
4 c. chicken broth
1/2 t. dried oregano
2 lg. bay leaves
1/2 t. salt
1/2 t. pepper
12-oz. pkg. noodles

In large pot, combine beans with their liquid, cover with water and bring to a boil, reduce heat and add olive oil, garlic, onion, celery, carrot, potato, tomatoes with juice, 2 cups of water and the chicken broth; bring to a boil. Add oregano, bay leaves, salt and pepper. Turn down the heat and simmer one to 2 hours. In a separate pan, cook noodles according to package directions. Drain and add to simmering soup. Makes 12 servings.

Get the whole family together on a chilly autumn day and take a hayride at a local pumpkin patch! After all the fun, warm up with some homemade soup!

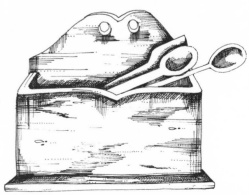

Creamy Pumpkin Soup

Penny Sherman
Cumming, GA

The addition of beef makes this pumpkin soup hearty and filling.

1 lb. beef short ribs	1 med. potato, peeled and cubed
2 T. oil	1 lg. carrot, chopped
4 c. water	1 med. onion, chopped
3 c. pumpkin, peeled, chopped	salt and pepper to taste

Brown short ribs with oil in a Dutch oven. Blend in water and bring mixture to a boil; reduce heat and simmer, covered, one hour. Remove short ribs from Dutch oven, cut off meat and shred; set aside. Stir in pumpkin, potato, carrot, onion, salt and pepper. Simmer, covered, for 45 minutes. Pour half of the mixture into a blender and combine until smooth; repeat with remaining half of soup; stir in reserved beef. Return to Dutch oven and heat before serving. Serves 6.

All of the sweet reminders of family and friends should be enjoyed. Fill a dry sink or side board with bowls of grandma's rag balls, cookie cutters or thimbles, baskets of children's blocks or toys and lots of family photos.

Soups

Hunting Cabin Chili

Wendy West Hickey
Pittsburgh, PA

This goes great with cornbread!

2 to 3 lbs. ground beef, browned
1 lg. onion, chopped
1 green pepper, chopped
1-lb. jar salsa
30-oz. can light red kidney
 beans, drained

3 15-1/2 oz. cans dark red
 kidney beans, drained
28-oz. can whole, peeled
 tomatoes
1/8 t. hot pepper sauce
salt to taste

Combine ingredients in a large soup pot. Tomato liquid should just almost cover ingredients or a little water can be added. Bring to a boil and reduce to low heat; simmer 2 to 3 hours.

Beef & Bacon Chowder

Tamara Ahrens
Davenport, NE

You can cook the carrots and potatoes in the microwave to save time!

1 lb. ground beef
2 c. celery, diced
1/2 c. onion, diced
2 10-3/4 oz. cans cream of
 mushroom soup
4 c. milk
3 to 4 c. potatoes, cooked and
 peeled

2 c. carrots, cooked and sliced
2 t. salt
1 t. pepper
12 bacon slices, crisply cooked
 and crumbled

Brown ground beef with celery and onion until meat is done and vegetables are tender. Place all ingredients in a saucepan; bring to a boil. Reduce heat and simmer until heated through.

Autumn leaves of russet, gold and red are pretty scattered down the center of a buffet table...add some acorns, too!

Shrimp Gumbo

Lorry Bates
Coshocton, OH

Even though my daughters are grown, they still request this recipe!

2 garlic cloves, chopped
2 onions, chopped
1 to 2 green peppers, chopped
2 T. margarine
16-oz. can tomatoes
12-oz. pkg. sliced okra pieces
16-oz. can tomato sauce
3 c. chicken broth

1 T. Worcestershire sauce
1 t. salt
1 t. chili powder
1 t. dried basil
1/4 t. pepper
bay leaf
1-1/2 lbs. salad shrimp
3 c. rice, cooked

Combine garlic, onions and green peppers in margarine and cook in a Dutch oven over medium heat until tender. Break tomatoes up with a wooden spoon; add to Dutch oven. Stir in okra, tomato sauce, broth, Worcestershire sauce, salt, chili powder, basil, pepper and bay leaf. Heat to boiling, reduce heat. Simmer, uncovered, for 45 minutes. Stir in shrimp, cover, and simmer for 5 more minutes. Remove bay leaf. Spoon hot rice into bowls, ladle gumbo over, stir before serving.

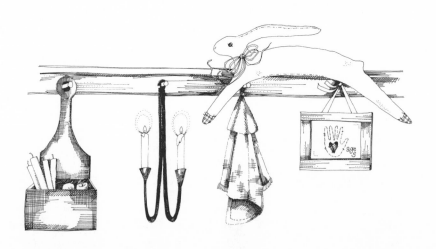

Soups

Corn Chowder

Louise McConnell
Reno, NV

*Spoon this creamy soup into a thermos to keep you toasty
during the next home football game!*

1/4 lb. bulk sausage	1 bay leaf
2 T. onion, diced	1 t. salt
3 c. milk	1 t. pepper
2 c. potatoes, cubed	1-1/4 c. cream-style corn

Cook sausage in a Dutch oven until thoroughly browned; remove and set aside. Sauté onion in drippings until tender; blend in milk, potatoes and bay leaf. Simmer 20 minutes then add remaining ingredients and sausage. Serves 6.

Herbs from your garden look wonderful hanging from peg boards, window sills, old drying racks or along your mantel. Hang several bundles in the kitchen too for adding to favorite soups and stews!

Crazy Quilt Potato Salad

Vickie

A colorful potato salad that will be a hit at any gathering!

9 c. red potatoes, cubed
1/2 c. onion, diced
1/2 c. celery, diced
1/4 c. sweet pickle relish
3 eggs, hard-boiled and chopped
1 garlic clove, minced

3/4 c. sour cream
1/3 c. mayonnaise
2 T. fresh parsley, chopped
1 t. dry mustard
3/4 t. salt
1/4 t. pepper

Add potatoes to a stockpot and cover with water. Bring to a boil. Cook 8 minutes or until tender. Drain; place in a large bowl. Add onion, celery, relish, eggs and garlic; toss gently. Combine sour cream and remaining ingredients; stir well. Pour over potato mixture; toss gently to coat. Cover and chill.

Corn Salad

Jackie Crough
Salina, KS

A nice change from regular salads! If you still have fresh corn in the garden, cook it and substitute for the canned.

17-oz. can yellow corn
17-oz. can white shoepeg corn
1/2 c. radishes, sliced
1/2 c. celery, chopped
1/2 c. green pepper, chopped

1 T. pimento
1/4 c. sweet relish
1/4 c. mayonnaise
salt and pepper to taste

Drain corn, mix with remaining ingredients in a large bowl. Stir well and refrigerate before serving.

✿ *Make whimsical Thanksgiving placecards! Take lots of pictures...football games, hayrides, raking leaves and trick-or-treating! Make color copies, cut out and glue to pieces of cardboard cut the same size.*

Salads

Turkey-Apple Salad

Liz Plotnick
Gooseberry Patch

Terrific for autumn picnics!

1 romaine lettuce head, torn
1 carrot, sliced
5 tomatoes, quartered
8 oz. smoked turkey, thinly
    sliced

4 apples, cored and sliced
2 T. cider vinegar
5 T. oil
1 T. Dijon mustard
Garnish: 1/3 c. walnuts, chopped

Toss together romaine, carrot, tomatoes, turkey and apples. Prepare dressing by blending together vinegar, oil and mustard. Add to salad and top with walnuts. Makes 8 servings.

Pull out all your favorites to welcome fall! Fill your open cupboards with brown crocks, redware and yellowware, bundles of wheat, beeswax candles and gourds. Line shelves with quilts or folded lengths of homespun in warm autumn colors.

Cauliflower & Broccoli Salad

Robbin Chamberlain
Worthington, OH

A popular salad gets a new twist...buttermilk dressing!

1 lg. cauliflower head, chopped
1 lg. broccoli bunch, chopped
1 green onion bunch, chopped
2 carrots, shredded
1 c. fresh peas, shelled

3/4 to 1 c. mayonnaise
1.4-oz. pkg. buttermilk salad
   dressing mix
2 T. sugar
2 T. vinegar

Combine and toss vegetables. Mix mayonnaise, salad dressing mix, sugar and vinegar. Pour over vegetables. Cover and chill overnight.

Apple Salad

Nikki Norman
Wheeling, MO

This recipe was handed down to me from my husband's grandmother, it's always requested and is a real treat!

3/4 c. water
1/4 c. vinegar
2 eggs
2 T. all-purpose flour

1 c. sugar
6 Golden Delicious apples,
   peeled, cored and chopped
6-oz. bag salted peanuts

Pour water and vinegar into a medium saucepan. Mix eggs, flour and sugar together in a bowl. Add to water and vinegar. Heat on high until boiling, stirring constantly. Reduce to medium heat and continue stirring until thickened. Remove from heat and set aside. Place apples and peanuts into large serving bowl, pour sauce over apples; toss.

Create a quick harvest centerpiece; it's easy! Set a straw wreath in the center of your dining table fill it with gourds and tuck a pillar candle in the center.

Cabbage-Chicken Salad

Vicky Grissom
Bakersfield, CA

One of my favorites!

1/2 c. vegetable oil
3 t. cider vinegar
3-oz. pkg. pork ramen noodles
    with seasoning packet,
    divided
3 T. sugar

1/2 t. salt
1/4 t. pepper
1 sm. cabbage head, shredded
6 green onions, chopped
4 chicken breasts, cooked and
    shredded

Mix together vegetable oil, vinegar, ramen noodle seasoning packet, sugar, salt and pepper. In large serving bowl, place cabbage, onions and chicken. Pour dressing over salad and mix. Crumble ramen noodles over the salad and toss salad until well mixed. Makes 8 servings.

Baskets with flat backs are perfect for your door...just slip them over the hook on a wreath hanger! They'll look lovely filled with colorful fall leaves, bunches of yarrow and dried sunflowers. Top your door with an autumn garland of grapevine and bundles of fresh bittersweet!

Rice Salad

Theresa Sutter
Tampa, FL

Not only a terrific rice salad, we've used this as a great stuffing for chicken breasts, too!

6-oz. box long grain and wild
    rice mix, cooked
4 oz. feta cheese, crumbled
1/2 c. green, yellow and red
    peppers combined, diced

1/2 c. onion, chopped
2/3 c. pine nuts, toasted
1/3 c. olive oil
2 T. white wine vinegar
1/8 t. pepper

Combine all ingredients, toss well and refrigerate at least 24 hours before serving.

Hot Potato Salad

Sharon Williamson
Baton Rouge, LA

My dear friend, Sharon, and I don't get to visit often, but when we do she knows I love her cooking...especially this recipe! It brings back memories of special times when our families had been together.

6 to 8 potatoes, peeled and diced
1 onion, chopped
1 t. mustard
1 c. mayonnaise

8-oz. pkg. pasteurized process
    cheese spread, cubed
Garnish: bacon bits

In large bowl, place potatoes, onion, mustard, mayonnaise and cheese. Combine well and spread into a buttered 2-quart baking dish. Top with bacon bits. Bake in a 350 degree oven for 30 minutes.

Black Bean Salad

Kay Sanderford
Victoria, TX

Choose a mild or hot picante sauce; either way it tastes great!

16-oz. can black beans, drained
  and rinsed
8-oz. can whole kernel corn,
  drained
4 oz. Monterey Jack cheese,
  cubed
3/4 c. green onions, sliced

3/4 c. celery, sliced
1 sm. red pepper, diced
3/4 c. picante sauce
1 T. olive oil
2 T. lemon juice
1 t. cumin
1 garlic clove, minced

Combine beans, corn, cheese, onions, celery and pepper in a large
bowl. Blend gently. Combine picante sauce, oil, lemon juice, cumin and
garlic; mix well. Toss with bean mixture and chill well before serving.

*...apples so red hang overhead, and nuts,
ripe-brown, come showering down in the
bountiful days of September.*

-Mary Howitt

Sweet Potato Crunch

Mike Rawl
Jacksonville, FL

Although sweet potatoes are easily stored in a cool, dry bin, they never seem to linger around our house because of this recipe!

3 c. sweet potatoes, cooked, peeled and mashed
1 c. sugar
1 stick plus 1/3 c. butter, melted and divided
2 eggs, slightly beaten

1 t. vanilla extract
1/3 c. all-purpose flour
1 c. brown sugar, packed
Garnish: 1 c. pecans, finely chopped

Mix sweet potatoes, sugar, one stick butter, eggs and vanilla. Place in a greased 2-quart baking dish. In separate dish, combine flour, remaining butter and brown sugar together. Spread flour mixture over sweet potato mixture. Sprinkle pecans on top. Bake at 350 degrees for 40 minutes.

❦ *Dress up windows with punched tin shutters; it's easy to create your own designs or copy stencil patterns. Just tape the stencil to the tin and use an awl and hammer to tap over the stencil design.*

Sides

Apple Cider Squash

Julie Miller
Gooseberry Patch

The perfect autumn combination!

1 lb. squash, peeled, seeded and
  chopped
1/2 c. apple cider
2 sm. apples, peeled and
  chopped

2 T. sugar
1/2 t. cinnamon
1/4 t. nutmeg
1 T. margarine

Combine squash and cider in a saucepan and cook until squash is tender; 10 to 15 minutes. Blend in remaining ingredients, cover, and cook 5 minutes longer.

Potato Strips with Cheese

Margaret Scoresby
Mount Vernon, OH

This recipe was shared with me when I was a newlywed.

4 med. potatoes
1/2 c. milk
1 T. butter
1 t. salt

pepper to taste
1/2 c. Cheddar cheese, shredded
1 T. dried parsley

Cut potatoes lengthwise into strips and place in a greased 8" square baking dish. Pour the milk over them, dot with butter and sprinkle with salt and pepper. Cover and bake for 45 minutes at 375 degrees or until potatoes are tender. Sprinkle with cheese and parsley and bake 5 minutes longer or until cheese is melted. Serves 4 to 5.

Scalloped Corn

Deanna Hershey
Powell, OH

A familiar favorite, no autumn dinner would be complete without it!

14-oz. can creamed corn
14-oz. can whole kernel corn,
    drained
1 t. salt
1/8 t. pepper
1 t. sugar

2 T. all-purpose flour
3 T. cream
1/2 c. milk
1 stick butter, melted
1-1/2 c. cracker crumbs

Mix corn with salt, pepper, sugar and flour. Add cream and milk. In separate bowl, combine butter and crackers; press half the mixture in the bottom of an 8" square baking dish. Add corn mixture and top with remaining crumbs. Bake at 375 degrees for 30 minutes. Makes 6 servings.

A good laugh is like sunshine in a house.

-Thackery

Homemade Applesauce

Sandy Benham
Sanborn, NY

I have applesauce with just about every meal...a great side dish!

10 tart apples, peeled, cored and
   chopped
3/4 c. brown sugar, packed
1/2 c. apple cider

1/8 t. nutmeg
1/8 t. salt
1-1/2 t. cinnamon

Combine all ingredients, cook over medium heat for 40 to 50 minutes.
Stirring occasionally.

Red Skin Mashed Potatoes

Kristi Hartland-Swartz
Gaithersburg, MD

A twist on an old favorite with sour cream and cream cheese, and
the addition of horseradish gives this side a kick!

8 to 10 lg. redskin potatoes,
   unpeeled and quartered
1/2 t. onion powder
salt to taste
1 T. prepared horseradish

8-oz. pkg. cream cheese,
   softened
1/2 c. sour cream, room
   temperature

Place potatoes in a large pot and cover with water. Bring to a boil.
Cook until potatoes are fork-tender, about 20 minutes; drain. Mash
potatoes and add remaining ingredients. Mix until fluffy; serve.

Grandma Herrmann's Dressing

Marilyn Borcharding
Waterloo, IL

For me, this recipe simply says "Grandma."

1 lg. yellow onion, diced
1 celery stalk, diced
1 stick butter
1-1/2 to 2 lbs. ground chuck
1-1/2 oz. pkg. dry onion soup
   mix

1 loaf bread, toasted and broken
   into cubes
2 eggs
10-3/4 oz. can cream of
   mushroom soup
salt and pepper to taste

Sauté onion and celery in butter. Add meat and onion soup mix, continue to cook until beef is thoroughly browned. In a very large bowl, place bread cubes, onion, celery, meat; mix well. Mix in eggs and cream of mushroom soup. Salt and pepper to taste. Bake in a 13"x9" well buttered pan. Place in a 350 degree oven for approximately 55 to 60 minutes. Check every 15 to 20 minutes, if cooking too quickly add more soup or gravy.

A collection of mismatched napkins, doilies or hankies can quickly become pretty shelf liners!

Sides

Vicki's Carrots

*Mary Davis
Clinton, NY*

Each year for the past 15 years, my best friend, Vicki, and I have gotten together to grind garden-fresh horseradish for this recipe!

6 to 8 carrots, peeled
1/4 c. water
2 T. onion, grated
2 T. horseradish
1/2 c. mayonnaise

1/2 t. salt
1/4 t. pepper
1/2 c. breadcrumbs
2 T. butter
1/8 t. paprika

Slice carrots in half, cut into thirds and place in a shallow, one-quart baking dish. In medium bowl, whisk together water, onion, horseradish, mayonnaise, salt and pepper. Pour horseradish mixture over carrots. In small bowl, combine breadcrumbs, butter and paprika. Top carrot mixture with breadcrumbs. Bake at 375 degrees for 35 to 40 minutes. Makes 4 servings.

Gingered Cranberry Sauce

*Tina Wright
Atlanta, GA*

Great served with ham or turkey.

8-oz. can jellied cranberry sauce, cubed
3/4 c. French salad dressing
1 T. soy sauce

1 t. ginger
1 t. garlic powder
1/8 t. cayenne pepper

Blend all ingredients together in a saucepan and simmer until cranberry sauce melts, stirring often. Let cool before serving. Makes 1-1/2 cups.

Use Shaker boxes to hold your favorite recipe cards.

Escalloped Apples

Jennifer Heinl
Pittsburgh, PA

An old-fashioned dish that goes great with any meal!

1/2 c. butter
2 c. fresh bread crumbs
4 med. tart apples, peeled, cored
  and sliced

1/2 c. sugar
1/4 t. cinnamon
1/4 t. cloves

Melt butter in a saucepan; add bread crumbs and toast lightly for about 2 minutes; set aside. Toss apples with sugar, cinnamon and cloves. In an oiled 8" baking dish, layer half of the apples and half of the toasted bread crumbs. Repeat with the remaining apples and bread crumbs. Bake at 325 degrees, covered, for 45 minutes or until apples are tender.

A wooden cookie tree can hold more than cookies! Tiny pumpkins and gourds are easily tied on with strands of jute...just use an awl to make a small hole in the end of a gourd or through the pumpkin stem and slip the jute through.

Cranberry Chutney

Pam Vienneau
Derby, CT

This will be yummy served with your holiday turkey dinner!

1-lb. can pineapple chunks
2 c. sugar
1 c. golden raisins
1/2 t. cinnamon
1/2 t. salt

1 lb. cranberries
1/4 t. ginger
1/2 t. allspice
1 c. nuts, chopped

Drain juice from pineapple and add enough water to make one cup liquid. In a large saucepan, combine with next 7 ingredients and simmer for 20 to 25 minutes; add pineapple and nuts. Pour chutney into sterilized jars, leaving 1/4-inch head space; seal. Process in a boiling water bath for 15 minutes. Yields six 8 ounce jars.

October's poplars are flaming torches lighting the way to winter.

-Nova S. Bair

Hash Brown Potato Casserole

Lorry Bates
Coshocton, OH

This tasty side dish is always a favorite! If you'd like, you can easily substitute an equal amount of frozen O'Brien potatoes...the added green pepper and onion are great!

8 oz. sour cream
2 lbs. frozen hash browns
1/2 stick margarine
10-3/4 oz. can cream of
  mushroom soup

10-3/4 oz. can cream of chicken
  soup
2 c. Cheddar cheese, grated
1 c. corn flake cereal, crushed

Mix all ingredients together except corn flake cereal. Bake in a 13"x9" pan at 375 degrees for 45 minutes. Cover top with crushed corn flake cereal and bake 15 minutes.

We often decorate our mantels, but why not show off your favorites around the hearth? Candles tucked in tiny terra cotta pots, punched tin lanterns, bunches of Indian corn or wheat and plump pumpkins look pretty grouped together in a cozy corner.

Sides

Wild Rice Stuffing
Vickie

Dates and crunchy almonds make this stuffing recipe special!

1-1/3 c. wild rice
2 T. butter
2 c. onion, chopped
1 c. carrots, grated
1 c. green pepper, chopped
6 c. unseasoned bread crumbs
1 c. slivered almonds

1/2 c. fresh parsley, chopped
10-oz. pkg. pitted dates,
  chopped
1-1/2 t. dried rosemary
1-1/2 t. dried thyme
1-1/2 t. dried sage
2 c. chicken broth

Prepare rice according to package directions; set aside. Combine butter, onion, carrot and pepper in a saucepan and sauté until onion is transparent; remove from heat. Blend in remaining ingredients, stir in rice. Spoon stuffing into a greased 13"x9" baking pan and bake at 325 degrees, covered, for 45 minutes. Remove cover and bake an additional 15 minutes. Makes 10 cups.

❧ Create a clever headboard...a distressed section of picket fence, a garden gate, trellis or old-fashioned feed sacks tacked to plywood!

Mom's Country Fried Steak

Sandy Dodson
Indianapolis, IN

*In the 1960's this main dish was my mother's special Sunday meal.
Our family couldn't wait to get home after church to sit
down to Mom's delicious afternoon supper.*

2 lbs. round steak
1/2 c. plus 1 T. all-purpose flour,
  divided
salt and pepper to taste

1 med. onion, chopped
1 sm. green pepper, chopped
1 T. vegetable oil
1 T. browning sauce

Cut steak into medium serving pieces. Place each piece between 2
pieces of wax paper and using a meat pounder, pound lightly. Place
1/2 cup flour into a plastic bag, along with salt and pepper to taste.
Place each piece of steak in plastic baggie to coat. Place steak, onion,
pepper and oil in a skillet and cook on low to medium heat until
the steak is cooked thoroughly on
both sides. Remove steak from
skillet and place on paper towels
to remove any excess fat. In the
skillet, with the drippings, add
one tablespoon of flour, salt
and pepper until the mixture is
blended. Slowly add water until
mixture thickens to desired
consistency; stir in browning
sauce. Add steak to gravy and
simmer on low heat for
approximately 45 minutes to
one hour. Salt and pepper to
taste. Makes 5 servings.

*Autumn...a time of harvest,
of gathering together.*

-Edwin Way Teale

Ham Steak & Brown Sugar Apples — Jo Ann

A simple and tasty home-cooked meal.

2 T. butter
1/4 c. brown sugar, packed
2 T. country-style mustard

2 med. tart apples, sliced
1-lb. ham steak

Melt butter in skillet; blend in brown sugar and mustard. Stir in apples and simmer until apples are just tender; 5 to 8 minutes. Spoon out apple mixture; set aside. Place ham steak in skillet and top with apple mixture. Over medium heat, cook, covered, until ham is thoroughly heated and done, 5 to 10 minutes.

Glazed Turkey Breast — Robbin Chamberlain, Worthington, OH

When you don't have a large crowd coming, just make a turkey breast for Thanksgiving dinner. This recipe is really good!

1 turkey breast, seasoned with
  salt and pepper
2 T. vegetable oil

1/2 c. apricot preserves
1 T. Dijon mustard
2 T. honey

Place turkey breast on a rack in a 13"x9" roasting pan. Drizzle oil over breast and bake in a foil tent at 325 degrees for 25 minutes per pound, or until meat thermometer registers 170 degrees. Combine remaining ingredients and glaze meat. Cook, uncovered, the final 30 minutes of cooking time, basting often.

Make tiny topiaries from herbs harvested from your garden.

Country-Style Ham Loaf

Lynn Williams
Muncie, IN

You can make several loaves ahead of time and freeze them. It's great to be able to just pop one in the oven for a quick homestyle dinner.

3 T. butter, melted	1 lb. ground ham
6 T. brown sugar, packed	1/2 lb. ground pork
2-1/2 t. dry mustard, divided	3/4 c. bread crumbs
1/8 t. cloves	2 eggs, beaten
4 pineapple slices	1/2 c. milk

In a mixing bowl, combine butter, brown sugar, 1/2 teaspoon dry mustard and cloves; blending well until brown sugar and mustard have dissolved. Pour mixture in a 9"x4" glass loaf pan, turning to coat the bottom. Lay pineapple slices in bottom; set aside. Blend ham, pork, bread crumbs, eggs, milk and remaining mustard. Shape into a loaf and place over pineapple slices. Bake at 350 degrees for one to 1-1/2 hours.

Line game boards along your stairway or in a keeping room...they'll add a whimsical touch!

Shepherd's Pie

Mary Rose Kulczak
Temperance, MI

A tasty way to turn leftover pot roast into a hearty meal!

10-oz. bag frozen mixed
   vegetables
1 to 2 c. pot roast, cooked and
   cubed
1 sm. onion, diced
12-oz. jar beef gravy

8-oz. can sliced mushrooms,
   drained
salt and pepper to taste
3 c. mashed potatoes
2 T. margarine

Prepare mixed vegetables according to package directions. Combine with next 5 ingredients and spoon in a 2-quart casserole dish. Spread mashed potatoes on top and dot with margarine. Bake at 350 degrees for 30 minutes.

Beef Tips & Noodles

Ann Hayes
Annville, PA

An easy recipe that only takes a few minutes to prepare!

3 10-3/4 oz. cans cream of
   chicken soup
1 t. dried parsley
salt and pepper to taste

1 T. onion, chopped
2 lbs. extra lean beef tips
2 12-oz. pkgs. bowtie pasta
   noodles

Stir first 5 ingredients together in a slow cooker. Place setting on low and let cook for 8 to 9 hours. Prepare noodles according to package directions; spoon beef tips over noodles.

Barbecue Hamburger

Mary Ann Clark
Indian Springs, OH

This recipe was one my mother used to make when I was just a young girl. After I left home and was married, I was thrilled to happen across the recipe!

1 c. celery, diced and cooked
1 c. carrots, coarsely grated and cooked
2 lbs. hamburger
2 onions, chopped
2 T. vinegar
1 t. salt

1/2 t. pepper
2 T. mustard
1 c. catsup
2 T. Worcestershire sauce
1/4 t. chili powder
2 T. all-purpose flour
2 T. brown sugar, packed

Combine celery and carrots in a saucepan, cover with water and cook until tender; set aside but don't drain. Brown meat with onions, stirring constantly. Combine all ingredients together, including carrots and celery with water. Let mixture simmer for 1/2 hour or until most of water has evaporated. Stir mixture occasionally and serve on hamburger buns.

Fold lengths of homespun on shelves to add a warm, old-fashioned feeling to your rooms.

Chicken & Vegetable Bake

Gail Hageman
Albion, ME

A warm and filling family dish!

1/2 c. all-purpose flour
salt and pepper to taste
1 T. paprika
2-1/2 lbs. boneless chicken
   breast, cut into serving sizes
2 T. shortening
1 onion, chopped
1/2 c. carrots, chopped

3-oz. can mushrooms, drained
1 T. brown sugar, packed
1/4 t. ginger
3 oz. frozen orange juice
   concentrate
3/4 c. water
3 to 4 c. rice, cooked

Combine flour, salt, pepper and paprika. Coat each piece of chicken with flour mixture. Reserve 2 tablespoons of remaining flour mixture. Brown chicken in shortening. Place chicken in a 2-quart baking dish and sprinkle with onion, carrots and mushrooms. Blend reserved flour mixture, brown sugar, ginger and salt into drippings. Stir to make a smooth paste. Add orange juice concentrate and water. Cook until bubbly. Pour over chicken and vegetables. Cover and bake at 350 degrees for 1-1/2 hours. Serve over rice.

October is crisp days and cool nights, a time to curl up around the dancing flames and sink into a good book.

−John Sinor

Mom's Pot Roast

Ronnie Ott
Mandeville, LA

A family favorite served with red cabbage, carrots or green beans!

1/4 c. all-purpose flour	1 sweet onion, chopped
1 T. plus 2 t. salt	2 10-3/4 oz. cans tomato soup
1-1/4 t. pepper	2-1/2 T. molasses
4-lb. pot roast	1/4 c. soy sauce
2 T. shortening, melted	1/8 t. ginger

Stir together flour, salt and pepper. Rub mixture into meat. Place shortening and meat in large skillet. Brown meat over medium heat, about 15 minutes. In medium bowl, combine onion, tomato soup, molasses, soy sauce and ginger. Place meat in Dutch oven and cover with sauce. Cook, covered, in 325 degree oven for 2-1/2 hours.

When the weather turns cooler, guest rooms need special touches...an extra quilt at the foot of the bed, a mug and thermos of warm spiced cider and flannel sheets to snuggle into.

Oven-Roasted Turkey

Mary Murray
Gooseberry Patch

Don't forget the homemade gravy and mashed potatoes!

15-lb. whole turkey
2 T. lemon juice
2 T. lime juice
1/4 c. turkey broth

1/4 c. brown sugar, packed
1-1/2 t. salt
1/2 t. pepper

Rinse turkey well; dry with paper towels. Combine lemon and lime juices, turkey broth and brown sugar; set aside. Place turkey in a shallow roasting pan; sprinkle with salt and pepper. Tuck a meat thermometer into the thickest part of thigh or breast, being careful that it doesn't touch bone. Roast the turkey at 325 degrees for 15 minutes per pound or 3-3/4 hours. During the last hour of roasting, baste the turkey with drippings in the pan to keep it moist; during the last 30 minutes, baste with brown sugar mixture. Make a tent of foil and place over turkey; continue to roast until meat thermometer reads 170 degrees in the breast meat and 185 degrees in the thigh. Place turkey on a warm platter and cover loosely with foil. Let rest 15 minutes before carving.

Sugar Cream Pie

*Betty Watson
Delaware, OH*

A good old-fashioned recipe.

1 c. sugar
1/8 t. salt
3 T. cornstarch
1 c. half-and-half

1/2 c. whipping cream
8-inch pie crust
Garnish: nutmeg

With wire whisk, mix sugar, salt and cornstarch. Add half-and-half and cream. Mix until sugar is dissolved. Pour into pie shell. Bake at 425 degrees for 15 minutes, then reduce heat to 350 degrees and bake 30 more minutes. Sprinkle with nutmeg. Cool before serving.

Pecan Munchies

*Randi Daeger
Rockford, IL*

Every year before Thanksgiving my mother managed to have at least 40 dozen cookies baked and in the freezer for the holidays! Of all her recipes, this is the one I like most and wanted to share.

1 c. pecans, chopped
1 c. butter, softened
1/2 c. powdered sugar
2 t. vanilla extract

1 T. water
2 c. all-purpose flour
6-oz. pkg. chocolate chips
Garnish: sugar

Spread pecans in a single layer on a cookie sheet and toast at 375 degrees for 5 minutes; watch carefully. Set aside to cool. Cream the butter and powdered sugar together until light and fluffy. Add vanilla and beat again. Thoroughly mix in the water and flour, then add chocolate chips and pecans. Shape into small balls, approximately 2 teaspoons of dough each. Place on an ungreased cookie sheet and bake in a preheated 300 degree oven for about 20 minutes. While still warm, roll cookies in sugar and place on cookie rack to cool.

Desserts

Banana-Walnut Upside Down Cake

Judy Clark
Jacksonville, FL

So popular in the 1950's, this moist and delicious cake is still great!

1/4 c. walnuts, coarsely chopped and toasted
1 c. brown sugar, packed
1/4 c. plus 6 T. unsalted butter, divided
3 T. pure maple syrup
4 lg. ripe bananas, peeled and sliced
1 c. all-purpose flour

2 t. baking powder
1/2 t. cinnamon
1/4 t. salt
3/4 c. sugar
1 lg. egg
1/2 t. vanilla extract
6 T. milk
Garnish: sweetened whipped cream

Toast walnuts by placing them on a cookie sheet and baking for 5 minutes at 375 degrees; watch closely. Set aside to cool. Combine brown sugar and 1/4 cup butter in heavy medium saucepan. Stir over low heat until butter melts and mixture is well blended. Pour in a 9" cake pan with 2-inch high sides. Spread to coat bottom of pan. Pour maple syrup over sugar mixture. Sprinkle walnuts evenly over top. Place banana slices in circles on nuts, overlapping slightly and covering bottom. Stir flour, baking powder, cinnamon and salt in medium bowl to blend. Beat sugar and remaining butter in an additional bowl until creamy. Add egg and vanilla; beat until light and fluffy. Beat in flour mixture alternately with milk. Spoon batter over bananas and bake at 325 degrees for about 55 minutes. Transfer cake to rack and run a knife around pan sides. Cool on rack for 30 minutes. Place plate over pan; invert cake, let stand 3 minutes, then gently lift off pan. Serve warm with whipped cream.

Asters, deep purple,
a grasshopper's call;
today is it summer,
tomorrow is fall.

-Edwina Falls

Pumpkin Patch Pie

Barbara Tuve
Montvale, NJ

Fun to make, fun to eat and puts a smile on everyone's face!

1-1/2 lb. pumpkin
1 to 2 apples cored, peeled and
   sliced
1/4 c. raisins
1/2 c. sugar

2 t. cinnamon
1 t. nutmeg
1/8 t. ginger
1/8 t. cloves

Wash the pumpkin, cut off top and clean out. Fill with apple slices, raisins, sugar and spices, mix well and place on cookie sheet to catch spills. Bake at 375 degrees for 1-1/2 hours or until apple slices and pumpkin flesh is fork tender. Serves one.

Baked Candy Apples

Kristy Boulds
Eldorado, IL

My mom always made these while we were growing up. Now, when we all get together at Mom's, the smell of the apples baking makes us feel like we're kids again.

2 c. sugar, divided
1 c. corn syrup
15 lg. Red Delicious apples,
   peeled and halved

brown sugar to taste
9-oz. pkg. red hot candies
3 to 4 drops red food coloring

Fill a large stockpot halfway with water, add one cup of sugar and corn syrup; stir well. Place apples in pot and let boil for 15 minutes. Butter a jelly roll pan; set aside. Take apples out of pan, reserving syrup mixture, and lay in jelly roll pan; sprinkle with brown sugar. To syrup mixture, add remaining cup of sugar, red hot candies and food coloring. Bring to a boil and pour over apples. Bake at 350 degrees for one hour. Makes 12 servings.

Desserts

Pennsylvania Dutch Muffin Cake

Gail Hageman
Albion, ME

*You can freeze this cake and it will still taste great
and be moist...just warm before serving!*

2 to 3 T. dry bread crumbs,
    crushed
2 c. plus 3 T. all-purpose flour,
    divided
1 T. baking powder
1/2 t. baking soda
1 t. salt
1-1/2 t. cinnamon, divided

1/2 t. allspice
1/4 t. cloves
1-1/2 c. sugar, divided
1/4 c. plus 2 T. butter, divided
1 c. sour cream
2 eggs
1 c. apples, peeled and grated

Butter an 8-cup soufflé dish and sprinkle with bread crumbs; tapping out excess. Combine 2 cups flour, baking powder, baking soda, salt, 1-1/4 teaspoon cinnamon, allspice, cloves, 1-1/4 cup sugar and blend well. Melt 1/4 cup of butter. Cool and stir in sour cream and beat in eggs. Beat the butter mixture into the dry ingredients and blend until the batter is smooth and satiny. Stir in apple. Spoon batter into prepared baking dish; smooth to level. Combine remaining sugar, flour and cinnamon; cut in butter, until mixture is crumbly. Sprinkle over batter. Bake at 350 degrees for one hour or until crumbs are lightly browned and a toothpick inserted comes out clean. If tube pan is used, test for doneness after 45 minutes. Cool in pan for 20 minutes, running a knife along the side of the pan. Remove from pan and cool on rack.

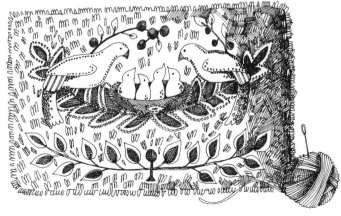

Harvest Sweet Potato Pie

Karen Stoner
Delaware, OH

An old-fashioned favorite; try it for Thanksgiving this year!

1-1/4 c. sweet potatoes, mashed
1/2 c. brown sugar, packed
1/2 t. salt
1/4 t. cinnamon
1/8 t. nutmeg
2 lg. eggs, lightly beaten

1/2 c. plain yogurt
1/4 c. milk
1 T. unsalted butter, melted
9-inch pie crust
Garnish: pecan halves, whipped
cream

Blend together sweet potatoes, brown sugar, salt, cinnamon and nutmeg. Whisk together eggs, yogurt, milk and butter; blend into sweet potato mixture. Spoon into pie crust and place pecan halves around edge of pie. Bake at 400 degrees for 45 minutes or until the crust is golden and the center is set. Makes 8 servings.

Children's toys bring back fond memories and smiles! Set a well-loved Teddy bear, pull toy, log cabin or doll on a trunk or tucked in a candle box.

Pumpkin Cheesecake Bars

Kim Henry
Library, PA

The first time I made these they disappeared in one evening;
now when I make them, I make 2 or 3 batches!

16-oz. pkg. pound cake mix
3 eggs, divided
2 T. margarine, melted
4 t. pumpkin pie spice, divided
8-oz. pkg. cream cheese

14-oz. can sweetened condensed
   milk
16-oz. can pumpkin
1/2 t. salt

In large bowl, combine cake mix, one egg, margarine and 2 teaspoons pumpkin pie spice until crumbly. Press into bottom of jelly roll pan. In large bowl, mix cream cheese until fluffy. Beat in sweetened condensed milk, pumpkin, salt, remaining eggs, and pumpkin pie spice. Mix well. Pour over crust. Bake at 350 degrees for 30 to 40 minutes. Cool and refrigerate before serving.

*Don't forget window
ledges and sills!
Tin animal silhouettes,
small corn husk wreaths,
twig stars, old apocathary
jars filled with rosehips or
buttons...all fond reminders
of grandma's house.*

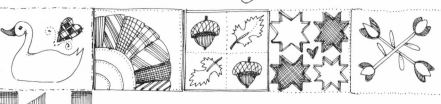

Autumn

🌰 **Make a garland of fall leaves;** *it's easy! Just string an embroidery needle with fishing line and push through the center of dried leaves until your garland is as long as you'd like. Drape it over your front door or around your windows for a colorful fall welcome!*

🌰 **Grandma's collection of bright green** handled kitchen utensils will look nostalgic displayed in an old dough bowl. Surround them with bunches of bittersweet and tiny ears of Indian corn.

🌰 **A hollowed out pumpkin** makes a perfect vase for a bouquet of homegrown marigolds, sunflowers and zinnias. Dress it up by cutting a scallop along the pumpkin's rim.

🌰 **Fill different size terra cotta pots** with florist's foam, then tuck in a bundle of wheat or rye. Tie a raffia bow around the bundle and hide the foam with moss…wonderful on your Thanksgiving buffet table!

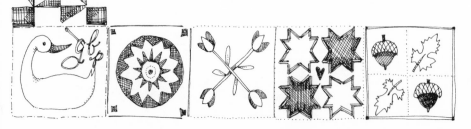

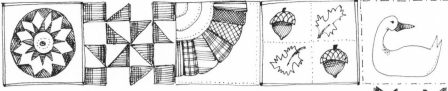

Autumn

🌰 **Rows of canning jars filled** with colorful homegrown goodies like corn, pickles, tomatoes, green beans, jams and jellies add a harvest feel to any cupboard! Top jar lids with corn husks and wrap with a raffia bow.

🌰 **Enjoy a harvest get-together** with family and friends! Serve hearty vegetable soup in a large hollowed out pumpkin, assorted sandwiches cut in festive Halloween shapes, taffy apples and spiced cider. Bob for apples, have a sack race, friendly pumpkin judging, then end the day with a hayride and bonfire!

🌰 **The simplest decorations** are often the best. Sunflowers hanging to dry from a peg rack, a dry sink lined with homespun and filled with squash, gourds and tiny pumpkins. Make a centerpiece of whatever flowers have dried in your garden...hydrangea, autumn leaves, bittersweet and black-eyed Susan.

🌰 **Make a beautiful harvest potpourri.** Combine slices of dried mini pumpkins, acorns, ears of baby Indian corn, sunflower petals and autumn leaves...beautiful!

acorns scarecrows football

School

Spiced cider

Thankfulness

hayrides

fires warm gats Trick·or·Treat

winter

Cherry Bacon Roll-Ups

Nancy Flanagan
Littleton, CO

Try this different type of appetizer, we think you'll really like it!

1/2 c. butter	2 eggs, beaten
1 c. water	1/4 lb. ground beef
1/2 c. dried cherries	1/4 lb. hot bulk sausage
2 c. herb seasoned stuffing mix	1 lb. bacon slices, cut into thirds

In a saucepan, melt butter in water; remove from heat. Combine cherries with stuffing. Mix butter and water mixture with cherries and stuffing in a large bowl. Blend well; chill one hour. Add remaining ingredients except bacon, mixing well. Shape into pecan-shaped balls; wrap with bacon, secure with toothpicks and place in a baking dish. Bake at 375 degrees for 35 minutes or until bacon is crisp. Makes 6 dozen.

❄ *Baskets add a handmade touch wherever you use them. Fill one with kindling and set next to the fireplace, or tuck a small evergreen or feather tree in a tall basket.*

Mozzarella-Bacon Snacks

Lisa Watkins
Gooseberry Patch

You can also make this with pepper bacon and sharp Cheddar or Swiss cheese if you'd like a different taste...be creative and try lots of different combinations!

12-oz. pkg. bacon
1 loaf frozen bread dough, thawed
2 t. olive oil

1 c. mozzarella cheese, shredded
1-oz. pkg. ranch salad dressing mix

Cook bacon until done, but not crisp. Cut into one-inch pieces and set aside. Roll bread loaf out into a 1/2-inch thick rectangle. Lightly brush the top with olive oil and cut dough into one-inch pieces. Combine bread dough, bacon, cheese and ranch salad dressing mix; toss to coat bread. Place dough mixture on an ungreased cookie sheet and using hands, gently shape into an oval loaf. Set aside until dough has risen to double in bulk. Bake at 350 degrees for 20 to 30 minutes or until lightly golden brown.

Use nature's bounty for wintertime decorations. Evergreen boughs wrapped with a rusty star garland draped along a fence, old-fashioned kissing balls made from mistletoe, a bowl of pinecones and ivy tucked under a bell jar or terra cotta pots overflowing with paperwhites.

Artichoke Appetizer

Phyllis Peters
Three Rivers, MI

My husband and I attended an Army reunion several years ago and were treated to the finest of southern hospitality. The veterans and their wives came from various parts of the country and we enjoyed sharing memories and delicious food. This recipe was given to me by Gladys, the wife of my husband's Army buddy.

28-oz. can artichoke hearts
1 c. grated Parmesan cheese
1 c. mayonnaise
1/8 t. garlic salt

1/8 t. Worcestershire sauce
1/8 t. hot pepper sauce
1/8 t. dried dill weed
Garnish: dried or fresh parsley

Drain and chop artichoke hearts. Combine with next 5 ingredients and blend well. Spoon onto lightly greased one-quart casserole dish. Sprinkle lightly with dill. Bake at 350 degrees for 20 minutes. Garnish with parsley. Serve on toast points, chips or crackers. Makes 3 cups. Serve hot or cold.

Make your bedroom a cozy spot to curl up in during the frosty winter. Quilts and coverlets are perfect to snuggle under during a nap, and a chair you can really settle into could be tucked in a corner. Don't forget a footstool and a basket filled with some of your favorite books!

Appetizers

Bacon-Wrapped Scallops

Robyn Wright
Delaware, OH

This is an elegant and tasty appetizer for a New Year's Eve gathering!

1/2 c. all-purpose flour
1/2 t. salt
1-1/2 t. paprika
1/2 t. white pepper
1/2 t. garlic powder

1 egg
1 c. milk
21 scallops
1 to 2 c. bread crumbs
7 bacon slices, cut into thirds

Combine flour, salt, paprika, white pepper and garlic powder in shallow dish. Beat egg and milk together in small bowl. Roll scallops in seasoned flour; shaking off excess. Dip scallops in egg mixture, then coat with bread crumbs. Preheat oven to 400 degrees. Wrap each scallop with bacon and secure with toothpick. Place scallops on lightly greased cookie sheet. Bake until bacon is crisp and scallops are cooked, about 20 to 25 minutes. Serve hot with remoulade sauce.

Remoulade Sauce:

4 T. lemon juice
4 T. red wine vinegar
4 T. horseradish
1 t. salt
1/2 t. pepper
1/2 c. cocktail sauce

2 t. paprika
1/8 t. cayenne pepper
1/2 c. mayonnaise
1/2 c. celery, minced
1/2 c. green onions, minced
4 T. mustard

Mix all ingredients together in a quart jar; shake well and chill for 45 minutes.

When there is room in the heart,
there is room in the house.

–Danish proverb

Cranberry Meatballs

Cathy Hurley
Poca, WV

My favorite appetizer because they travel well to any potluck dinner or church social, and they're usually the first to disappear!

2 eggs, beaten
1 c. corn flake cereal, crushed
1-1/3 c. catsup, divided
2 T. soy sauce
1 T. dried parsley flakes
2 T. dried onion
1/2 t. salt

1/4 t. pepper
2 lbs. ground unseasoned pork
16-oz. can jellied cranberry
  sauce
3 T. brown sugar, packed
1 T. lemon juice

In a mixing bowl, combine eggs, crumbs, 1/3 cup catsup and next 6 ingredients; shape into 72 one-inch meatballs. Place in a 15"x10" baking pan. Bake at 350 degrees for 20 to 25 minutes or until done. Remove from the oven, drain meatballs on paper towels. In a large saucepan, combine cranberry sauce, brown sugar, lemon juice and remaining catsup. Simmer until cranberry sauce is melted; stirring often. Add the meatballs and heat through.

✳ *Top your mantel with nostalgic items...candle molds, game boards, children's blocks; a Shaker box with a Teddy bear peeking out and an old sampler...all these can quickly be tucked among greenery.*

Mr. Snowman Cheeseball

Jan Sofranko
Malta, IL

This little guy is so adorable, everyone will want one of their own!

2 8-oz. pkgs. cream cheese
4-1/2 oz. jar dried beef, diced
1 green onion bunch, chopped
1/2 t. garlic powder
1 t. horseradish

1/2 c. dried parsley
8-oz. tub whipped cream cheese,
Garnish: black olives, baby
    carrots, dried cranberries and
    pretzel sticks

Mix both packages of cream cheese with dried beef. Add green onions; blend in garlic powder and horseradish. Form into 2 balls and roll each in dried parsley and stack one on top of the other making the bottom larger than the top ball. Spread the whipped cream cheese as frosting on the snowman. Break off irregular pieces of a black olive to form 3 buttons down the front, the mouth and 2 eyes; use the tiny carrot for the nose. Wrap the green onion tops around the neck for a scarf and tie. Use rosemary sprigs or pretzel twigs for the arms. Make a halo on his head from the dried cranberries. Serve with biscuits or other hearty crackers.

Everywhere, everywhere, Christmas tonight!

-Phillip Brooks

Crab Meltaways

Pamela Geib
Cordova, MD

This recipe is easy and so delicious! I don't know anyone who doesn't enjoy it and I always have requests to share the recipe!

2 8-oz. jars sharp pasteurized process cheese spread	1 t. garlic salt
1 stick butter	1 lb. crab meat
	6 English muffins, halved

Combine cheese, butter and garlic salt in saucepan over low heat until mixture is completely melted. Remove from heat; add crab meat and mix thoroughly. Spoon mixture onto the 12 muffin halves. Broil until golden brown. Cut muffins into quarters.

Christmas! Tis, the season for kindling the fire of hospitality in the hall, the genial fire of charity in the heart.

—Washington Irving

Sesame Chicken Wings

Leekay Bennett
Delaware, OH

*The black beans and ginger give these wings a nice change
from other recipes you've probably tried.*

12 chicken wings
1 T. black beans
1 T. water
1 T. oil
2 garlic cloves, crushed
2 fresh ginger slices, shredded

3 T. soy sauce
1-1/2 T. rice wine
1/8 t. pepper
1 T. sesame seeds
Garnish: green onions

Discard chicken wing tips and separate wings into 2 pieces. Mash beans with a ricer or the back of a fork and combine with water; set aside. Add oil to a deep skillet and stir in garlic and ginger; add the chicken wings. Cook over medium heat, stirring occasionally, until wings are lightly browned. Blend in soy sauce and wine and continue to cook 30 seconds longer. Add black beans and pepper and simmer, covered, 8 to 10 minutes. Uncover skillet and turn temperature to high. Continue to cook, stirring continually until liquid is almost evaporated. Remove skillet from the heat and sprinkle on sesame seeds, stir to coat wings. Garnish with green onions before serving. Serves 6.

❋ *You can make swag holders from small
wreaths tucked into the corners of your windows!*

Grandma Bailey's Buns

Doris Myers
Marysville, WA

A family recipe for over 75 years. My mother-in-law, who raised 10 children and cooked for a dozen farmhands on a Minnesota homestead, found that this was expected at all gatherings.

1 c. hot mashed potatoes
3/4 c. shortening
2 eggs, beaten
1 t. salt
1/4 c. sugar

5 c. all-purpose flour, divided
1/2 pkg. active dry yeast
1/4 c. warm water
1 c. milk, scalded and cooled to
  lukewarm

Blend potatoes, shortening, eggs, salt and sugar. Stir in 2 cups flour. Dissolve yeast in water, blend into potato mixture. Stir in cooled milk and remaining flour. Knead until smooth adding enough flour not to be sticky. Place in a warm greased bowl. Cover with cloth and let raise in a warm place, about 2 hours. Punch down and knead onto lightly floured surface. Form dough into small baseball size rolls and place on greased cookie sheet. Let dough rise until double in bulk. Bake at 400 degrees for 10 minutes then reduce temperature to 350 degrees and bake an additional 15 minutes. When light brown, remove from oven and butter tops.

✳ *Punched tin lanterns cast a soft glow when you hang them on your porch or fence posts. Fill old tins with water and freeze solid. Use an awl to tap a design on the outside, don't forget to make 2 holes for hanging. Just let the ice melt, slip a length of wire through the 2 holes and set a pillar candle inside!*

Buttery Crescent Rolls

Robin Hill
Rochester, NY

*These flaky crescents will melt in your mouth! Try them
topped with homemade jam and real butter!*

1/2 c. milk
1 stick butter, softened
1/3 c. sugar
1/2 t. salt
1 pkg. active dry yeast

1/2 c. warm water
2 eggs, lightly beaten and
   divided
3-1/2 to 4 c. all-purpose flour

Heat milk until bubbles form; set aside. Blend together butter, sugar
and salt; stir in hot milk and let mixture cool to lukewarm. Dissolve
yeast in warm water, set aside for 5 to 10 minutes, then beat yeast
mixture with one egg and stir into milk. Add 2 cups of flour and
continue beating until mixture thickens. Stir in enough remaining flour
until dough begins to pull away from the sides of the bowl. Knead
dough on a lightly floured surface for 2 to 3 minutes. Place dough in
an oiled bowl, turning once to coat. Let rise in a warm place until
double in size, about one hour. Punch down dough and divide in half;
let dough halves rest for 10 minutes. Roll one half of the dough into a
12-inch circle, cut each into 6 pie-shaped triangles. Beginning at large
end, roll up each triangle. Place on a lightly oiled baking sheet and
slightly curve ends to form crescent shape; repeat with remaining
dough. Cover crescents and let rise again 30 minutes. Brush crescents
with remaining beaten egg and bake at 400 degrees for 15 minutes.
Makes one dozen rolls.

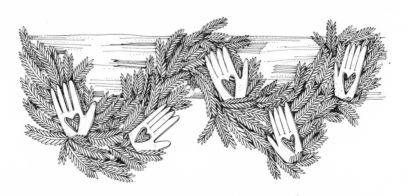

Christmas Trees

Susan Young
Madison, AL

Pretty served with a holiday dinner or topped with a tasty spread.

1 c. grated Parmesan cheese
1 c. Monterey Jack cheese,
  shredded
1-1/2 c. all-purpose flour
1 stick cold, unsalted butter,
  cubed

1/2 t. salt
1/2 t. cayenne pepper
1 T. ice water
1 lg. egg, slightly beaten
Garnish: dried parsley flakes and
  grated Parmesan cheese

Preheat oven to 350 degrees. Using a blender or food processor, mix cheeses, flour, butter, salt and cayenne pepper until blended. Add water and mix rapidly until dough leaves sides of bowl. Divide dough into thirds and roll out one piece at a time on lightly floured rolling surface to 1/8-inch thickness. Cut out with Christmas tree cookie cutter; place on ungreased cookie sheet. Brush with egg; sprinkle with desired amounts of Parmesan cheese and parsley flakes. Bake for approximately 8 to 9 minutes or until bottoms are golden. Cool one minute and remove to racks.

O Christmas tree,
O Christmas tree,
how true you
stand unchanging!

-German folk song

Lemon-Glazed Eggnog Loaf

Emily Jordan
Delaware, OH

Great to wrap up and give to a neighbor, or enjoy a slice with a cup of herbal tea after a busy day of holiday shopping!

2 c. all-purpose flour
1 c. sugar, divided
1 T. baking powder
1/2 t. salt
1/2 t. nutmeg

1 egg
3 T. vegetable oil
1 c. eggnog
1/4 c. lemon juice

Combine flour, 2/3 cup sugar, baking powder, salt and nutmeg in a mixing bowl. In a small bowl, beat egg, then whisk in oil and eggnog. Make a well in the center of the dry ingredients and pour in the egg mixture. Stir by hand just until all flour particles are moistened. Turn into a greased and floured 9"x5" loaf pan; bake at 350 degrees for 50 to 60 minutes or until tester comes out clean. Meanwhile, combine lemon juice and remaining sugar in small saucepan. Bring to a full boil, stirring until sugar is dissolved. As soon as the bread is removed from the oven, poke holes down through the bread using a long wooden skewer. Slowly spoon on the hot glaze until all of it is absorbed. Cool bread for 10 minutes in pan, remove to wire rack.

Make ice candles to light the way to your home. Fill several small buckets or pint-size milk cartons with water and set in your freezer. As the water freezes from the outside in, the center will still be hollow. Turn them upside down, set a votive inside and nestle your ice candle in the snow!

My Grandmother's Graham Bread

The Governor's Inn
Ludlow, VT

As this bread bakes and the aroma fills your kitchen, try to imagine another era when bread was baked every day. We recommend that you double the recipe, as it has a way of disappearing!

2 c. milk
2 T. cider vinegar
1-1/2 c. graham flour
2 c. all-purpose flour

1/2 c. brown sugar, packed
1/2 c. molasses
2 t. baking soda
1 t. salt

Combine milk and cider vinegar; let stand 5 minutes. Blend all ingredients together until thoroughly combined, either by hand or using a heavy-duty mixer. Pour batter into 2 greased 9"x5" loaf pans. Bake at 350 degrees for 30 minutes.

Flavored Butter

Kara Allison
Dublin, OH

So good on a thick slice of still-warm homemade bread.

1/2 c. butter, softened
2 T. seedless blackberry jam
1/3 c. pecans, finely chopped

In a small bowl, blend together butter, jam and pecans. Refrigerate, covered, for 8 hours before serving to allow flavors to blend.

Personalize glass ornaments to give as party favors!

Breads

Christmas Fruit Bread

Candy Hannigan
Monument, CO

Try a slice spread with cream cheese...wonderful!

1/2 c. butter
1 c. brown sugar, packed
2 eggs
2 lg. bananas, mashed
1 lg. apple, peeled and grated
1 T. orange zest

2 c. all-purpose flour
3/4 t. baking soda
3/4 t. baking powder
1/2 t. salt
1 c. dried cranberries

Cream butter and brown sugar together; beat in eggs. Stir in mashed bananas, apple and orange zest. In separate bowl, combine flour, baking soda, baking powder and salt; stir in banana mixture. Add cranberries until just blended. Bake in a greased 9"x5" loaf pan at 350 degrees for 40 minutes. Turn the pan on its side and cool 10 minutes. Remove from the pan and continue cooling on wire rack. Wrap in plastic wrap and serve the next day.

Summer fading, winter comes,
frosty mornings, tingling thumbs,
window robins, winter rooks,
and the picture story-books.

-Robert Louis Stevenson

Candy Canes

Jo Ann

Kids will love these...they're so cute for a holiday get-together!

1 pkg. active dry yeast
1/4 c. warm water
3/4 c. warm milk
1/4 c. sugar
1/4 c. shortening
1 t. salt
1 egg, lightly beaten
3-1/4 to 3-3/4 c. all-purpose flour, divided
1 c. red candied cherries, quartered
1 c. powdered sugar
1 T. milk

Add yeast to warm water; stir to dissolve. Blend in warm milk, sugar, shortening, salt, egg and 2 cups flour; beat until smooth. Fold in candied cherries; stir. Add enough remaining flour to form a soft dough. Knead dough on a lightly floured surface until smooth and elastic; about 6 to 8 minutes. Place in a greased bowl and turn to coat dough. Cover and let rise in a warm place until double in size, about one hour. Punch down, let rest 10 minutes and divide in half. Roll each dough half into a 12"x7" rectangle. Using a sharp knife or pizza cutter, cut 12 one-inch strips from each rectangle. Twist each strip and place on a lightly oiled baking sheet. Curve one end of each strip to look like a cane. Cover loosely with a cloth and let rise until double in size, about 45 minutes. Bake at 375 degrees for 12 to 15 minutes or until lightly golden brown; cool completely. Combine powdered sugar and milk and drizzle icing over rolls. Makes 2 dozen.

Open the lid of an old blanket chest or trunk and let all the memories tucked inside show! Layers of hand-stitched quilts, Teddy bears and dolls, buckle shoes or a little girl's tea set...all lovely reminders.

Angel Orange Rolls

Kathy Grashoff
Ft. Wayne, IN

On a chilly winter's morning, there's nothing like these rolls
still warm from the oven with the delicious
icing dripping down the sides!

1 loaf frozen sweet roll dough
3 T. margarine, melted and
   divided
1/4 c. sugar

1 t. cinnamon
1 c. powdered sugar
zest and juice of one orange

Thaw bread dough according to package directions and roll out on a
floured surface to a 14"x8" rectangle. Spread dough with 2 tablespoons
margarine, then sprinkle with sugar and cinnamon. Roll up dough
jelly-roll style and pinch ends to seal. Cut rolls into 1-1/2 inch pieces
and arrange in a 9" round baking dish coated with cooking spray.
Cover rolls and allow to rise about 2-1/2 inches high. Bake in 350
degree oven for 20 to 25 minutes. Combine remaining margarine,
powdered sugar, juice of one orange and orange zest. Spread frosting
over the rolls while warm.

Turn old quilt scraps into a
special ornament for friends.
Cut a 6-inch star pattern on
heavy brown paper. For each
ornament, cut 2 stars from the
scraps. Stitch right sides
together leaving a 2 inch
opening at the top. Turn right
side out, fill with batting and
slip stitch closed. Make a loop
of ribbon and sew to the top of
the ornament.

Potato Bread

Cheri Maxwell
Gulf Breeze, FL

There's nothing like old-fashioned potato bread.

3 med. potatoes, peeled and
   sliced
1 T. active dry yeast
1 T. sugar

1/2 c. warm water
1 c. potato-cooking water
4 to 6 c. all-purpose flour
1 t. salt

Place potatoes in a saucepan, cover with water and boil until tender; about 20 minutes. Measure out one cup of water that the potatoes were cooked in; set aside and discard any remaining water. Mash potatoes and reserve 1-1/2 cups; use any remaining potatoes for another recipe. Combine yeast and sugar in warm water. Stir to dissolve yeast and let sit for 5 minutes or until mixture is foamy. Blend in potato cooking water, reserved mashed potatoes, 2 cups flour and salt. Beat mixture until well blended. Set aside, covered, and let rise for 45 minutes. Add enough of the remaining flour to form a stiff dough. On a lightly oiled surface, knead dough for 5 minutes. Place dough in an oiled bowl and turn to coat all sides of dough. Cover loosely and let rise until double in size, about one hour. Punch the dough down and shape into 2 loaves. Place dough in 2 lightly oiled 9"x5" loaf pans and let rise again until double in size. Bake at 350 degrees for 50 minutes to one hour, or until loaves sound hollow when tapped.

Breads

Easy Spoon Rolls

Gail Goudy
Walls, MS

A family favorite, we always make this during the holidays.

1 pkg. instant dry yeast
2 c. hot water
1-1/2 sticks margarine, melted
1/4 c. sugar
1 egg, beaten
4 c. self-rising flour

Dissolve yeast in water; set aside. Cream margarine and sugar; add egg and combine with yeast. Add flour and stir until well mixed. Place dough in bowl with a tight fitting lid and refrigerate until ready to use. Dough will remain fresh in the refrigerator for several days. Drop by heaping teaspoonfuls into oiled muffin tins and bake at 350 degrees for 15 to 20 minutes. Makes 18 to 24 rolls.

Jars of home-grown vegetables bring cheer sitting side-by-side on cupboard shelves. Red tomatoes and green beans look festive alongside apples and evergreen boughs. Send a jar home with each of your holiday guests.

Steve's Clam Chowder

Dana Stewart
Gooseberry Patch

My little brother fixes this for all of his out-of-town guests and it never fails to impress!

5 bacon slices, crisply cooked
    and crumbled, drippings
    reserved
2 med. potatoes, finely chopped
1 celery stalk, finely chopped
1 carrot, finely chopped
1 onion, finely chopped
2 8-oz. bottles clam juice
2 t. chicken bouillon

1/2 t. salt
1/4 t. celery salt
1 t. dried thyme
pepper to taste
1-1/2 T. all-purpose flour
3 c. milk
1 c. cream
1 lb. clams

In a Dutch oven, add potatoes, celery, carrot and onion to bacon drippings and cook until softened, about 5 minutes. Add clam juice, chicken bouillon, salt, celery salt, thyme and pepper; simmer briefly. Mix flour with milk and cream in a jar with a tight-fitting lid; shake to blend and add to Dutch oven. Simmer until thickened and bubbly. Add clams and let cook 5 minutes longer; stir in bacon.

Christmas day should be fragrant with the love that we bear one another.

-Charles Dickens

Soups

Grammy's Cabbage Soup

Kate Conroy
Bethlehem, PA

In the winter, my grammy would make this soup and simmer it all day while we played outside; the delicious smell seemed to waft through the entire neighborhood!

2 to 3-lb. smoked pork shoulder
1 lg. onion, sliced
4 to 6 qts. water
3 to 4 potatoes, peeled and diced
2 14-1/2 oz. cans whole tomatoes, drained and chopped

1 sm. cabbage head, shredded
1 t. dried parsley
1 t. dried basil
salt and pepper to taste
Garnish: 1 garlic clove, minced

In a 10 to 12-quart stock pot, cook pork and onion in water for about one hour to make stock. Add potatoes, tomatoes, cabbage, parsley and basil. Simmer for one to 2 hours longer, adding salt and pepper. After pork is cooked, remove, shred and return to soup. If desired, sprinkle garlic on top before serving. Makes 8 to 10 servings.

Invite friends over for a Soup Supper during a frosty winter afternoon or evening. Ask everyone to bring their favorite soup or bread to share, as well as good company! You provide the bowls, spoons and a crackling fire.

Cream of Chicken Soup

Wendy Paffenroth
Pine Island, NY

We love this creamy soup with a salad and crusty French bread.
It really takes the chill out of a winter's evening.

4 to 5-lb. chicken
2 celery stalks, diced
2 carrots, diced
1 med. onion, diced
1 c. orzo, cooked
1 c. cake flour

1-1/2 c. cold water
2 c. milk
salt to taste
pepper to taste
dried parsley to taste
garlic powder to taste

Place chicken in a stockpot, cover with water and boil until chicken juices run clear when pierced. Remove meat from bone and return to stockpot. Add celery, carrots and onion to broth. Bring to a simmer and add orzo to broth; bring to a boil. Blend cake flour and cold water, stir until smooth and add to the broth when it boils. Add milk and simmer until soup thickens, stirring often. Add salt, pepper, parsley and garlic powder.

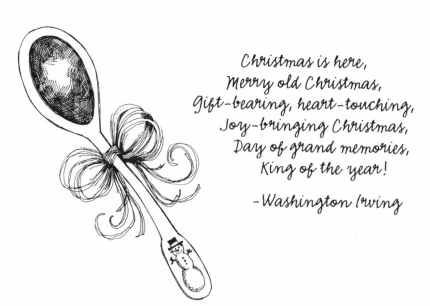

Christmas is here,
Merry old Christmas,
Gift-bearing, heart-touching,
Joy-bringing Christmas,
Day of grand memories,
King of the year!

-Washington Irving

Creamy Potato Soup

Karen Gillespie
Marion, OH

I'm a restaurant chef and this is one of our guests' favorite soups...that is if the staff doesn't get to it first!

1 med. onion, chopped
1-1/2 c. plus 1 to 2 T.
    butter-flavored oil
10 potatoes, cubed
3 qts. water
2 t. salt
1 to 2 c. all-purpose flour

2 qts. heavy cream
1 lb. bacon, crisply cooked and
    crumbled
pepper to taste
Garnish: Cheddar cheese,
    shredded and green onions,
    chopped

Sauté the onion with one to 2 tablespoons butter-flavored oil; set aside. Place potatoes in water and bring to a boil, cook until tender but not falling apart. Don't drain potatoes. Stir in sautéed onions and salt; set aside. Blend together remaining butter-flavored oil and enough flour until consistency is thick and batter-like. It's important to slowly add the flour and oil mixture to hot potatoes and water so as not to create lumps or break up potatoes too much; mixture will be thick. Add cream, bacon and pepper. Gradually heat the soup without boiling the cream. Garnish with Cheddar cheese and green onions.

Baby hemlocks that have been tucked into terra cotta pots are just the right size to decorate a side board, dry sink or place setting. Top them with some sphagnum moss to keep them from drying out.

French Market Soup

Virgina Smalls
Charleston, SC

This would make a great gift for neighbors! Just fill a canning jar with the bean soup mix, write the recipe on a pretty card and tie on with a strand of raffia.

2 c. 13-bean soup mix
1 ham hock
1-1/4 t. salt
1/4 t. pepper
2 qts. water

16-oz. can spiced tomatoes
1 lg. onion, chopped
1 garlic clove, minced
1 chili pepper, chopped
1/2 c. lemon juice

Place beans in a Dutch oven and cover with water 2 inches above beans. Let beans soak overnight, or bring to a boil and cook for 2 minutes. Remove from heat, cover, and let stand for one hour. Combine ham hock, salt, pepper and 2 quarts of water. Bring to a boil, reduce heat and add drained bean mix. Let simmer 1-1/2 hours or until beans are just tender. Add remaining ingredients and let simmer 30 minutes. Remove ham hock, chop meat and return to soup before serving.

It's impossible to describe the beautiful effect of firelight and candlelight...the smell of greens and woodsmoke is delicious. In the stillness of that first glimpse, one of the canaries will often trill into song.

—Tasha Tudor

Soups

Homestyle Bean Soup
Vickie

Hearty and filling, this is ready to enjoy in less than 15 minutes!

2 T. garlic, minced
2 T. olive oil
12-oz. can tomato paste
2 15-oz. cans pinto beans,
    undrained
2 T. fresh parsley, chopped

2 14-1/2 oz. cans chicken broth
salt and pepper to taste
3-1/2 c. hot water
1/2 c. shell pasta
Garnish: fresh Parmesan cheese,
    grated and fresh parsley

Sauté garlic in oil until tender. Blend in tomato paste, beans and parsley. Stir well and simmer 2 minutes. Blend in chicken broth, salt, pepper and water; bring to a boil. Add pasta and simmer until tender; 8 to 10 minutes. Garnish with Parmesan cheese and parsley.

Winter's snow can dust even your mailbox with magic. Put a smile on your postman's face and turn yours into a gingerbread house! Sprigs of evergreen, tiny windows, even a roof of shingles. Don't forget to leave a treat inside, too!

Crunchy Salad Almondine

Jackie Crough
Salina, KS

Very pretty for a special holiday luncheon or buffet table!

1/4 c. butter
1/2 c. slivered almonds
1 lettuce head, chopped
2 c. celery, chopped
2 T. fresh parsley, chopped
2 c. green onions, chopped
2 11-oz. cans mandarin
    oranges, drained

1/2 c. oil
1/2 t. hot pepper sauce
1/4 c. sugar
1 t. salt
1/8 t. pepper
1/4 c. tarragon vinegar

Melt butter in a saucepan, add almonds and toast lightly; about
2 minutes; set aside to cool. In a large serving bowl, combine lettuce,
celery, parsley, green onions, mandarin oranges and almonds; refrigerate until ready to serve. Combine oil, hot pepper sauce, sugar, salt,
pepper and tarragon vinegar; whisking well. Pour over salad just
before serving.

❄ *Put a small tree*
somewhere unexpected so
it will be "discovered" by
family and friends...on
a stairway landing,
inside an open cupboard
or on a dry sink!

Salads

Red & Green Slaw

Zoe Bennett
Columbia, SC

This colorful salad is perfect for a Christmas potluck and it's so easy to prepare.

6 c. cabbage, shredded
1/2 c. red onion, finely chopped
1/2 c. red pepper, sliced
1/2 c. green pepper, sliced
1/2 c. celery, chopped

2 T. sugar
1-1/2 t. salt
1/2 t. celery seeds
1/3 c. white vinegar
1/4 c. olive oil

Combine cabbage, onion, red pepper, green pepper and celery in a large serving bowl. Whisk together sugar, salt, celery seeds, vinegar and oil until thoroughly combined and sugar is dissolved. Pour dressing over cabbage; toss lightly. Refrigerate, covered, for 30 minutes to allow flavors to blend. Makes 6 to 8 servings.

❄ *Even the birds can have a festive house for the winter! Paint the sides of an unfinished birdhouse in any of your favorite country colors; let dry. Use a hot glue gun to glue mesquite wood chips on the the roof, or bend a vintage license plate and secure with epoxy. Tie a bow on a small wreath and glue around the birdhouse opening...your feathered friends will love their new home!*

Christmas Salad

Mable Covey
Sheridan, MI

*Just as my mother did, this is the only salad I prepare for Christmas.
I think it's beautiful served in a glass pedestal dish.*

10-1/2 oz. pkg. mini-
  marshmallows
15-1/4 oz. can sliced pineapple,
  drained
1/4 c. maraschino cherries,
  drained and halved
3 med. apples, sliced
3 med. bananas, sliced

8-oz. pkg. pitted dates
1/2 c. walnuts, chopped
1 sm. bunch seedless purple
  grapes
3 1/2 pts. whipping cream
1 t. vanilla extract
1/2 to 3/4 c. sugar
Garnish: whipping cream

Mix first 8 ingredients together. Whip the whipping cream, add the
vanilla and sugar. Pour over the salad and mix well.

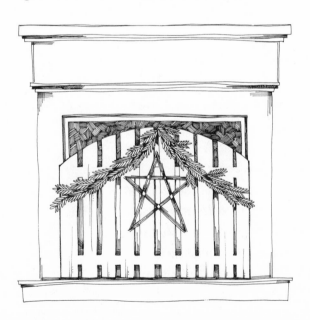

❋ *A fireboard can easily be made from a section of picket
fencing; add a simple evergreen swag and twig star.*

Salads

Cranberry-Pecan Salad

Megan Brooks
Antioch, TN

All the ingredients blend together to make this one of our favorites.

2 radicchio bunches, torn
1 red leaf lettuce bunch, torn
2 endive bunches, torn
1/2 c. dried cranberries
3 pears, thinly sliced
1/4 c. pecans, chopped
1/4 c. Gorgonzola cheese
1/3 c. pear juice
2 T. vinegar
4 T. oil
1 t. red onion, minced
2 T. lemon juice

In a large mixing bowl, combine radicchio, red leaf lettuce and endive. Toss salad greens with cranberries, pears, pecans and cheese; set aside. Before serving, whisk together pear juice, vinegar, oil, red onion and lemon juice; toss with salad.

Dreamy Orange Salad

Neta Liebscher
El Reno, OK

My husband's favorite!

6-oz. pkg. sugar-free orange
   gelatin
1 c. hot water
10-oz. can crushed pineapple
11-oz. can mandarin oranges
2 c. buttermilk
1/2 c. almonds, chopped
16 oz. whipped topping

Dissolve gelatin in water; refrigerate 30 minutes. Add pineapple, oranges, buttermilk and almonds. Chill until almost set, then fold in whipped topping.

These are the days that reindeer love!

-Emily Dickinson

Artichoke-Rice Salad

Marion Pfeifer
Smyrna, DE

Why not host a shopper's brunch for your friends? Serve this with assorted sandwiches, vegetables and fruit. Spend time chatting about your holiday plans...then head out for an afternoon of shopping together!

3 6-oz. jars marinated artichoke hearts
4 c. chicken broth
2 c. white rice, uncooked
5 green onions, chopped
4-oz. jar pimento-stuffed olives, sliced
1 green pepper, diced
3 celery stalks, diced
1/4 c. parsley, chopped
1 t. curry powder
2 c. mayonnaise
salt and pepper to taste

Drain, but reserve liquid from artichoke hearts; chop and set aside. In a stockpot, bring chicken broth to a boil; stir in rice. Simmer 20 minutes or until liquid is absorbed and rice is tender; cool. Add artichokes, onions, olives, green pepper, celery and parsley to rice; stir well. Combine reserved artichoke liquid with curry; blend in mayonnaise, salt and pepper. Stir with rice and vegetables, chill before serving.

❋ *Old shutters are perfect for showing off your holiday cards or nostalgic family photos.*

Salads

Crunchy Shrimp Salad

Kari O'Neill
Klamath Falls, OR

You can also substitute cooked chicken for the shrimp...yummy!

2 c. small shrimp, cooked
2 T. sesame seeds, toasted
1/2 c. almonds, toasted
1/2 head cabbage, chopped
2 green onions, chopped
3-oz. pkg. chicken ramen
    noodles with seasoning
    packet, divided

1 T. sugar
1 c. oil
1 t. pepper
4 T. vinegar
1 T. soy sauce
1 t. sesame oil

In large bowl, combine shrimp, sesame seeds, almonds, cabbage and green onions. Crumble ramen noodles and add to salad. Blend together remaining ingredients and pour over shrimp mixture; toss well.

Spaghetti Salad

Linda Zell
Delavan, WI

An easy salad you can prepare the night before!

1 lb. spaghetti, cooked and
    drained
2 cucumbers, peeled and diced
2 tomatoes, diced
3 to 4 green onions, diced

1/2 green pepper, diced
8-oz. bottle Italian salad
    dressing
2 T. salad seasoning

Combine all ingredients, tossing well to coat. Refrigerate several hours or overnight before serving.

Potato Sleighs

Phyllis Laughrey
Mount Vernon, OH

*You can always use Co-Jack or smoked Cheddar cheese, or top
your potato sleighs with fresh tomatoes and sour cream!*

4 med. potatoes, baked
1/2 c. sour cream
1/3 c. milk
3 T. butter
2 T. chives, chopped
1 t. salt

1/8 t. pepper
1-1/2 c. Cheddar cheese, grated
1 med. onion, minced
1/2 lb. bacon, crisply cooked and
    crumbled
paprika

Cut 1/3 off the top of each potato, scoop out potato and set aside;
discard the top shells. Scoop out potato from remaining halves leaving
1/4-inch thick shell. Mash potatoes with sour cream, milk, butter,
chives, salt and pepper. Spoon mixture into each shell and sprinkle
with cheese, onion, bacon and paprika. Return potato sleighs to oven
and bake at 350 degrees until heated through and cheese is melted.
Serves 4.

*Not believe in Santa Claus!
You might as well not
believe in fairies...*

-Frances P. Church

✳ Sides ✳

Cornbread Stuffing

Becky Sykes
Gooseberry Patch

*Using a cornbread mix makes this a quick holiday side dish; but
you really should try it with homemade cornbread, too!*

1/2 stick butter
2 lg. celery stalks, chopped
1 lg. yellow onion, chopped
7-oz. pkg. cornbread stuffing
    mix
4 bread slices, cubed

1/2 c. chicken broth
1/2 c. parsley, chopped
1 T. dried sage, crumbled
2 t. dried thyme, crumbled
1/2 t. salt
1/2 t. pepper

Melt butter in a large saucepan, add celery and onion and sauté until
vegetables are tender; about 10 minutes. Remove from heat and
gently stir in cornbread stuffing mix, bread cubes, chicken broth,
parsley, sage, thyme, salt and pepper. Spoon stuffing into a lightly
oiled 2-1/2 quart baking dish. Bake, covered, at 325 degrees for
45 minutes. Serves 12.

✳ *An old legend tells us the
Christmas stocking came about
when St. Nicholas tossed gold
coins down the chimney of three
sisters who needed a dowry. The
coins fell into the sisters'
stockings that happened to be
hanging on the fireplace to dry!*

Holiday Hash Browns

Tammy McCartney
Oxford, OH

I make these potatoes every holiday...the kids love them!

2 c. sour cream
2 c. Cheddar cheese, shredded
1/2 c. onion, chopped
10-3/4 oz. can cream of chicken
 soup

2-lb. pkg. frozen hash browns,
 thawed
1/2 c. margarine
2-1/2 c. crispy rice cereal

Mix together sour cream, cheese, onion and soup. Add hash browns to mixture. Place in a 13"x9" pan. Melt margarine and mix with crispy rice cereal. Spread on top of potatoes. Bake at 350 degrees for 55 minutes.

The Christmas bells from hill to hill,
answer each other in the mist.

-Alfred Lord Tennyson

Scalloped Vegetables

Diana Chaney
Olathe, KS

Add this old-fashioned dish to your family dinner.

3 c. celery, sliced
1/2 c. water
4-oz. can mushrooms, drained
10-oz. pkg. frozen peas, thawed
8-oz. can sliced water chestnuts, drained
10-3/4 oz. can cream of celery soup

1/2 t. seasoned salt, divided
1/2 t. dried savory, crumbled and divided
1/4 t. dried thyme, crumbled and divided
2 T. butter, melted
1/2 c. dry bread crumbs

Combine celery and water in a saucepan, simmer 5 minutes; drain. Blend celery with mushrooms, peas, water chestnuts and soup. Sprinkle in seasoned salt, half of the savory and thyme; mix well. Place vegetable mixture in an ungreased 1-1/2 quart casserole dish. Mix together butter, bread crumbs and remaining herbs; spoon on top of casserole. Bake, uncovered, at 350 degrees for 25 minutes.

❄ Who can forget the thrill of a downhill ride on a sled? If you come across a sled at a flea market, give it a home! Fill it with greenery or gifts, or rest alongside a cupboard.

Water Chestnuts & Barley

Kim Roepke
Omaha, NE

A family recipe from one of Mom's dear friends. Each time I prepare it, I think them both and all the fun they had together.

1 c. quick-cooking barley	4-oz. can sliced mushrooms
1/2 c. butter	8-oz. can sliced water chestnuts
1 sm. onion, chopped	1-1/2 oz. pkg. dry onion soup
2 c. chicken broth	mix

Combine barley and butter in a saucepan and brown lightly. Blend in onion, chicken broth, mushrooms, water chestnuts and dry onion soup mix; stirring until well blended. Spoon barley mixture into a 1-1/2 quart casserole dish and bake at 350 degrees for one hour.

❈ *A festive mitten filled with tiny goodies...wrapped squares of homemade fudge, caramels, a bag of mulling spices or cocoa mix and chocolate-covered spoons makes a wonderful surprise to slip on a neighbor's doorknob!*

❄ Sides ❄

Hazelnut-Mushroom Pilaf

Stephanie Moon
Green Bay, WI

This is always a favorite and it goes well with so many dishes!

1/2 c. hazelnuts, coarsely
   chopped
1/2 c. long grain rice, uncooked
1/4 c. orzo, uncooked
1/2 c. mushrooms, sliced
1/2 c. onion, diced

1/4 c. celery, finely chopped
1/4 c. butter
2 c. chicken broth
2 T. fresh parsley, chopped
1/4 t. dried marjoram
1/4 t. pepper

Spread hazelnuts in a single layer on a baking sheet and bake at 350 degrees for 8 to 10 minutes; stir and set aside to cool. In a large skillet, sauté rice, orzo, mushrooms, onion and celery in butter. Stir constantly and continue to cook until rice is lightly browned. Blend in broth, parsley, marjoram and pepper; bring to a boil. Reduce heat and simmer, covered, for 15 minutes. Remove from heat and let stand, covered, for 10 minutes before serving; stir in hazelnuts. Serves 4.

❄ *If you don't have a mantel, hang stockings on peg boards, bed posts or door knobs!*

Spicy Cranberry Sauce

Corrine Lane
Gooseberry Patch

This is a little spicier than traditional cranberry sauce, but adding honey, ginger and just a little cayenne pepper makes it really good!

1-3/4 c. cranberry juice cocktail, divided
1 T. orange zest
3/4 c. honey
1 cinnamon stick
1 t. fresh ginger, peeled and minced

3/4 t. coriander
1/2 t. salt
1/2 t. pepper
2 whole cloves
1/8 t. cayenne pepper
12-oz. bag fresh cranberries

In a saucepan, blend together 1-1/2 cups cranberry juice cocktail, orange zest and honey. Simmer 5 minutes to completely melt honey. Add cinnamon stick, ginger, coriander, salt, pepper, cloves and cayenne pepper; simmer 2 minutes longer. Stir in cranberries and continue to simmer until berries pop and sauce begins to thicken; about 10 to 20 minutes. Remove saucepan from heat and stir in remaining cranberry juice cocktail; blend well. Refrigerate until ready to serve. Makes 3 cups of cranberry sauce.

❋ Snow day? Gather your family together and play board games, look through family photo albums and watch a classic old movie. End your day together with a cozy picnic in front of the fire.

Old-Fashioned Broccoli & Onions

Vickie

A comforting dish in the wintertime; a real favorite.

3 1-lb. pkgs. frozen sm. whole
   onions
1 lb. broccoli flowerets
5 T. butter, divided
5 T. all-purpose flour
2 c. milk
1 c. whipping cream

salt and pepper to taste
1/2 t. Worcestershire sauce
1-1/2 c. Cheddar cheese,
   shredded
1/2 c. fresh bread crumbs
2 T. Parmesan cheese

Prepare onions according to package directions; drain and set aside. Place broccoli in a steamer or in the top of a colander over a pot of boiling water and steam until just tender; set aside. Melt 4 tablespoons butter in a saucepan and stir in flour, whisking constantly, until bubbly and thick. Blend in milk, whisking constantly, then add cream, salt, pepper and Worcestershire sauce. Bring mixture to a boil and continue to boil until mixture becomes thick, stirring constantly. Blend in cheese and continue to cook until cheese is melted. Stir onions and broccoli in cheese sauce, then spoon into 3-quart casserole. Melt remaining butter and toss with bread crumbs and Parmesan cheese; sprinkle over casserole. Bake at 375 degrees for 30 to 40 minutes, until bubbly and light brown.

❄ *Thread dried cranberries on wire, then gently bend into letters to spell Noel, love or joy. Slip strands of raffia between the cranberries, add a loop and hang in your window!*

Southern Peach Yam Bake

Rebecca Chrisman
Citrus Heights, CA

I love yams for Christmas dinner!

1/2 c. brown sugar, packed
3 T. all-purpose flour
1/2 t. nutmeg
2 T. margarine

1/2 c. pecans, chopped
2 17-oz. cans yams, drained
16-oz. can peach slices, drained
1-1/2 c. mini-marshmallows

Combine sugar, flour and nutmeg; cut in margarine until mixture resembles coarse crumbs; add nuts. Stir yams with peaches and spoon in a 1-1/2 quart casserole; sprinkle with sugar mixture. Bake at 350 degrees for 35 minutes. Sprinkle with marshmallows and broil until lightly browned.

Baked Shredded Carrots

Robin Wilson
Altamonte Springs, FL

This recipe is easy and tastes great...what more could you ask for?

12 c. carrots, shredded
3 T. sugar

3/4 t. salt
6 T. butter

Lightly toss together the carrots, sugar and salt until well combined. Spread evenly in 13"x9" casserole dish and dot with butter. Bake, uncovered, at 325 degrees for one hour.

❄ Sides ❄

Homemade Corn Pudding

Kathy Grashoff
Ft. Wayne, IN

*Try adding this simple side dish to your favorite meal...it's
a terrific comfort food for cozy winter suppers.*

3 eggs
2 c. corn
1/2 c. sugar
4 c. milk
1/2 t. cloves

1/4 t. nutmeg
1 T. all-purpose flour
1/2 t. salt
1/2 t. cinnamon

Beat eggs until light; add remaining ingredients and stir well. Pour into
a 13"x9" baking dish. Set in pan of hot water and bake, uncovered, at
350 degrees for 45 minutes. Serve hot.

❄ *Enjoy your favorite birdhouse collection all
winter long! Surround them with spruce branches
and strings of cranberries, hang tiny wreaths
or garlands on the doors.*

Ham Tetrazzini

Tammy McCartney
Oxford, OH

*Shared with me by a wonderful friend, this casserole
has become one of our favorites.*

1 c. ham, cooked and diced
2 T. onion, chopped
1 T. butter
10-3/4 oz. can cream of
   mushroom soup

1 c. Cheddar cheese, shredded
1 T. sherry
6 oz. spaghetti, cooked
1 T. fresh parsley, chopped

In saucepan, cook ham, onion and butter until onion is tender. Blend
in soup, cheese and sherry. Cook until cheese melts, stirring often. Add
spaghetti and parsley. Heat thoroughly and serve.

Fettuccine Alfredo

Cathie Lopez
La Mirada, CA

You can add shrimp or steamed vegetables to this recipe, too.

12 oz. fettuccine
1/2 c. butter
1/2 pt. half-and-half
1 t. white pepper

1/2 c. fresh Parmesan cheese,
   grated
1/2 t. salt

Prepare pasta according to package directions; set aside. Melt butter in
a saucepan; blend in remaining ingredients and heat through. Spoon
over noodles.

Swiss-Mushroom Chicken

Nikkole Koslowski
Columbus, OH

Quick and elegant!

3 whole skinless, boneless split
    chicken breasts
6 oz. Swiss cheese, sliced
1/4 lb. fresh mushrooms, sliced
1/2 c. chicken broth

10-3/4 oz. can cream of chicken
    soup
2 c. herbed stuffing mix
1 stick butter, melted

Place chicken breasts in a lightly oiled 13"x9" dish. Add a slice of cheese on top of each breast half, place mushrooms over cheese. Blend together broth and soup; spoon over chicken. Sprinkle stuffing mix on top and drizzle with melted butter. Bake at 350 degrees for 45 to 50 minutes or until juices run clear when chicken is pierced.

Frosty, in a coat of
red, with a scarf upon his
head. A ball of snow from
head to toe, before the
springtime he must go!

-Anonymous

Country-Baked Ham

Kim Henry
Library, PA

This is the best ham you'll ever have...it's always tender and guests are usually copying the recipe down before they go home!

5 to 8-lb. precooked ham
16-oz. can pineapple slices,
    drained
1-1/3 c. brown sugar, packed

2 t. dry mustard
1/4 c. bread crumbs
3 T. cider vinegar

Unwrap ham and wipe off with a damp cloth. Place in large pan with a small amount of water on the bottom. Using toothpicks, place pineapple slices across the top of ham. Mix together remaining ingredients and glaze the top of ham. Cover with foil and bake at 350 degrees for 20 minutes per pound. During the last 10 to 15 minutes, remove foil and increase oven temperature to 425 degrees. When done, meat thermometer inserted near the center should register 160 degrees.

It's fruitcake weather!

-Truman Capote

Glazed Cornish Hens

Geneva Rogers
Gillette, WY

*This is a wonderful recipe that's perfect anytime you
want to prepare a special dinner.*

1/3 c. sesame seeds, toasted
2/3 c. onion, chopped
2/3 c. celery, chopped
1/3 c. plus 3 T. butter, melted

2 t. poultry seasoning
3 c. rice, cooked
1 T. dried parsley
4 Cornish hens

Toast sesame seeds by spreading them on a baking sheet and baking
at 350 degrees for 8 to 10 minutes; stir and set aside to cool. Sauté
onion and celery in 1/3 cup butter until tender. Blend in poultry
seasoning, rice, parsley and sesame seeds. Spoon mixture into hens
and place breast-side up in a shallow roasting pan. Brush tops with
remaining melted butter and roast, uncovered, at 350 degrees for 30
minutes. Prepare glaze and brush over hens, continue to roast another
30 minutes, basting often.

Glaze:

1/3 c. sugar
1 T. cornstarch
1 t. coriander
1/4 t. lemon zest

1/4 t. onion powder
1/8 t. pepper
1-1/4 c. orange juice

Combine sugar, cornstarch and seasonings in a saucepan; blend
in orange juice. Bring mixture to a boil, reduce heat and simmer
until thickened.

Cranberry Pot Roast

Crystal Lappie
Worthington, OH

A flavorful, sweet and sour main dish.

16-oz. can tomato sauce
16-oz. can jellied cranberry
    sauce
1 t. horseradish
1 t. dry mustard

3 t. apple cider vinegar
1/4 c. cranberry juice
1 T. vegetable oil
3-lb. boneless chuck roast,
    trimmed

Combine tomato sauce, cranberry sauce, horseradish, mustard, vinegar, juice and oil in a Dutch oven and bring to a boil. Simmer, uncovered, 5 minutes. Place the roast into the pan with the sauce and cover. Simmer over low, basting every so often, for 2 to 3 hours, until meat is very tender. Transfer roast to a serving platter. Allow the sauce to cook down to desired thickness. Spoon some over the roast and save some as extra sauce. Cut roast across the grain into thick slices before serving. Makes 6 to 8 servings.

❄ Decorate your tree with out-grown mittens, socks and booties for a darling memory tree. A tiny bonnet or stocking cap will make a sweet tree topper!

MAINS

Maple Pork Chops

Vickie

*Have this for good luck on New Year's Day! Great served with
sauerkraut, mashed potatoes and homemade stuffing.*

4 pork chops
2 T. oil
1 Rome apple, chopped
1/4 c. golden raisins
1 T. butter
2 onions, sliced

1 t. fresh thyme, chopped
salt and pepper to taste
1/2 c. chicken broth
2 T. maple syrup
1 T. all-purpose flour

Brown pork chops in oil over medium heat. Place in a single layer in a
casserole dish and top with apple and raisins. Combine butter, onions,
thyme, salt and pepper in a saucepan and cook over medium heat
until onions are transparent; transfer to baking dish. Whisk together
chicken broth, maple syrup and flour until well blended. Pour chicken
broth and onion mixture over pork chops. Bake at 400 degrees for 30
minutes. Serves 4.

A merry Christmas to us all, my dears!

-Charles Dickens

Savory Mushroom Meatloaf

Karen Ray
Mission Viejo, CA

Whether served with mashed potatoes or sliced for a sandwich alongside a hearty bowl of soup...this never fails to be my favorite.

1 egg, beaten
1/2 c. milk
1 t. dried savory
1 t. salt
1/2 t. pepper
1-1/2 lbs. ground beef

1 c. butter crackers, crushed
3/4 c. mushrooms, sliced
3/4 c. Swiss cheese, grated
1/4 c. red onion, diced
2 bacon slices, cut in one-inch
  pieces

Blend together egg, milk, savory, salt and pepper. Add ground beef, crackers, mushrooms, cheese and red onion, mixing thoroughly with your hands. Shape into a loaf and place in a loaf pan. Place bacon slices on top and bake at 350 degrees for 50 minutes.

✳ *Enjoy lots of natural wintertime decorations...fill your fireplace opening with candles in every size and shape, top your mantel with red and green apples, pears, grapes, holly and balsam sprigs!*

Slow Cooker Beef Stroganoff

*Denise Guarni
Medford, NJ*

*This is one of my favorite recipes, because it's
always a comforting wintertime meal.*

1-1/2 lbs. stew beef
1 lg. onion, sliced
2 10-3/4 oz. cans cream of
   mushroom soup
2 T. catsup

2 t. Worcestershire sauce
1 t. pepper
1/2 to 1 pt. sour cream
12-oz. pkg. noodles, cooked

Place beef and onion in slow cooker. Mix soup, catsup, Worcestershire sauce and pepper together. Add to slow cooker; mixing well. Place on low setting for 8 to 10 hours. Just before serving, add sour cream and heat through. Serve over noodles.

✳ *An old window frame that's missing all the glass panes can become a clever country bulletin board...perfect for all the cards, letters and photos you receive during the holidays! Just nail chicken wire to the back of the frame and attach your holiday greetings to the wire mesh with paper clips.*

Mushroom-Spinach Crêpes

Julie Dobson
Loma Linda, CA

If you're looking for a special recipe for a cozy dinner,
these crêpes are easy to prepare and so good!

1/2 c. plus 4 T. butter, divided
4 c. milk
1/2 c. all-purpose flour
1/2 c. plus 4 T. grated Parmesan
cheese
2 c. mushrooms, sliced

4 T. green onion, chopped
2 8-oz. pkgs. cream cheese
2 eggs
3 c. frozen spinach, thawed and
drained
8 12-inch flour tortillas

Prepare white sauce by blending together 1/2 cup butter, milk, flour and 4 tablespoons Parmesan cheese; set aside. Sauté mushrooms and onions in remaining butter, add one cup of white sauce and set aside. Mix cream cheese, eggs, spinach and 1-1/2 cups of white sauce. Grease a 13"x9" pan. Spread bottom of pan with a thin layer of white sauce. Layer tortillas on top of white sauce, then spinach, then tortillas, mushrooms, tortillas, spinach, tortillas. Top with white sauce and 1/2 cup of Parmesan cheese. Bake at 350 degrees for 45 minutes. Serve warm.

❄ Create a snowman wreath; a whimsical door greeting! Tie three different sizes of wreaths together with heavy wire, then hide the wire with several strands of raffia. Don't forget to add a wire loop at the top for hanging, then just tuck twigs at each side for arms!

Prime Rib & Yorkshire Pudding

Donna Dye
London, OH

Each Christmas I use this recipe...I know I can count on it and it's truly perfect every time!

9 to 12-lb. rib roast
1-1/4 c. all-purpose flour,
    divided
1-3/4 t. salt, divided

pepper to taste
4 T. roast drippings
2 eggs
1 c. milk

Rub roast well with 1/4 cup flour, one teaspoon salt and pepper to taste, and place bone side down in a shallow roasting pan. Bake at 500 degrees and cook 15 minutes per rib. For example a 3-rib roast would bake 45 minutes, a 5-rib roast; one hour and 15 minutes; the oven will smoke. After cooking the designated time, turn off the oven and don't open the door for 2 more hours. Cooking your prime rib this way will give you a rare roast with a crispy outside. If you want your roast medium, just add 15 minutes to the total roasting time. Prepare Yorkshire pudding by adding roast drippings to an 11"x7" baking pan. Place pan in a 450 degree oven while preparing batter. Blend together eggs, milk, remaining flour and remaining salt until well blended. Pour into baking pan and bake 25 to 30 minutes.

❋ *An evergreen branch can be cut and "planted" in an old watering can. Add tiny candles and "snowflakes" of Queen Anne's lace.*

Seafood Lasagna

Christi Miller
New Paris, PA

For seafood lovers, this is a dream come true!

1/2 c. plus 2 T. butter
1/2 c. all-purpose flour
4 c. milk
salt and pepper to taste
3 T. olive oil
1 c. onions, chopped
1/2 c. grated Parmesan cheese
1 lb. med. shrimp, peeled,
    deveined and cooked
1 lb. bay scallops, cooked
2 lbs. fresh spinach, washed and
    stems removed
2 lbs. mushrooms, chopped
1-1/2 lbs. lasagna noodles,
    cooked
8-oz. pkg. cream cheese, cubed
2 lbs. mozzarella cheese
2 lbs. crabmeat, shredded

Prepare sauce by melting 1/2 cup butter in a large heavy pan over medium heat. Stir in flour and cook, stirring constantly. Do not brown. Remove from heat and gradually stir in milk. Return to heat and cook, stirring constantly with a wire whisk, until thick and smooth. You should have approximately 4 cups of sauce. Season with salt and pepper; set aside. In a large skillet, heat the olive oil over medium heat. Add onions and sauté; remove from heat. In a saucepan, combine onion with 3 cups of prepared sauce. Stir in Parmesan cheese, fold in shrimp and scallops; set aside. Steam spinach until tender; coarsely chop. Sauté mushrooms in remaining butter until tender and set aside. Oil the bottom of two 13"x9" pans. With remaining cup of sauce, spread a thin layer on the bottom of pan. Cover with a layer of noodles, spread 1/2 of seafood sauce over noodles, top with 1/2 of spinach, 1/2 of cream cheese, 1/4 of mozzarella cheese and 1/2 of crabmeat. Repeat layers beginning and ending with noodles. Spread on remaining sauce and top with mozzarella cheese. Bake, uncovered, at 350 degrees for 45 minutes or until bubbly. Let stand 10 minutes before serving.

The only gift is a portion of thyself.

-Ralph Waldo Emerson

MAINS

Gift-Wrapped Chicken

The Governor's Inn
Ludlow, VT

We think this makes a beautiful presentation; just like a package!

4 boneless, skinless chicken
   breasts
16-oz. can whole berry
   cranberry sauce

8 T. butter, divided
16-oz. pkg. phyllo dough,
   defrosted in refrigerator
1/2 c. butter, melted

Cut each chicken breast in half the short way and pound each piece to lightly flatten. Place one tablespoon cranberry sauce and one tablespoon butter on each piece of chicken breast and place another breast piece on top; repeat with remaining chicken. Cut dough in half the long way. Brush melted butter on 4 pieces of dough. Stack cut strips of dough to make a star shape; just layer 2 strips to make an "x" then add the remaining 2 on top to form a "+". Place filled chicken in center of your dough star and pull ends up together in the center, pinching them closed at the top like a beggar's purse. Bake at 375 degrees for 25 minutes. Serves 4.

❊ Make a homemade snowglobe! Just glue a ceramic or plastic figure in the lid of a small jar using clear-drying epoxy; let dry. Fill the jar almost to the top with distilled water, then add some glitter and a little glycerin. Tightly screw the lid on the jar and turn...let it snow!

Warm Cinnamon Pudding Cake

Cindy Watson
Gooseberry Patch

There's nothing like warm gingerbread and cinnamon together!

2-1/2 c. all-purpose flour
1-1/2 t. baking soda
1-1/4 t. ginger
1 t. cinnamon
1/2 t. salt
1/2 t. allspice
1/4 t. nutmeg

3/4 c. butter, softened and
  divided
1/2 c. sugar
1 egg
1 c. molasses
3 c. hot water
3/4 c. brown sugar, packed

Blend together flour, baking soda, ginger, cinnamon, salt, allspice and nutmeg; set aside. Cream together 1/2 cup butter and sugar; beat in egg until well combined. Stir in flour mixture, adding alternately with molasses and one cup water. Pour into 13"x9" baking pan and sprinkle top with brown sugar. Combine remaining butter and water; mixing well. Pour on top of batter; don't stir. Bake at 350 degrees for 40 to 55 minutes. Cake will crackle. Serve warm. Makes 12 servings.

✳ *Enjoy a wintry day of play with your children! Bake and decorate cookies, make snow ice cream, build a snow fort or cut out paper snowflakes.*

Desserts

Chocolate-Oatmeal Cookies

Sherri Smith
Lucedale, MS

These are quick and easy to make!

2 c. sugar
3 T. cocoa powder
1/2 c. butter
1/2 c. milk

1/2 c. creamy peanut butter
1/4 t. vanilla extract
3 c. quick oats

Mix together sugar and cocoa in a saucepan. Add butter and milk over medium high heat. Bring to a boil for one minute. Remove from heat. Add peanut butter and vanilla; mixing well. Slowly add quick oats, making sure all oats are covered. Drop by spoonfuls onto wax paper and wait a few minutes while they harden.

Cranberry Squares

Susan LeBlond
New Canaan, CT

So pretty for a cookie exchange!

2 c. cranberries, halved
1/3 c. walnuts, chopped
1-1/2 c. sugar, divided
1 egg
2 T. butter, melted

4 T. safflower oil
1 c. all-purpose flour
1/8 t. salt
1/2 t. vanilla extract

Spray a 9" square baking pan with non-stick spray. Mix cranberries, walnuts and 1/2 cup of the sugar. Spread evenly in baking pan. Mix together remaining sugar and remaining ingredients. Stir until smooth and pour over cranberry mixture. Bake at 350 degrees until top crust is a light golden brown, about 40 minutes. Cool for at least 30 minutes. Cut into 3-inch squares.

Laugh and be merry together!

-John Masefiled

Tea Party Carrot Cookies

Mel Wolk
St. Peters, MO

This is a favorite cookie recipe from my mother. It makes the most delicate little cookies, not overly sweet...perfect for tea.

3/4 c. shortening
3/4 c. sugar
1 egg
2 c. all-purpose flour
2 t. baking powder
1/2 t. salt
3 to 4 carrots, peeled, cooked
   and mashed

1-1/2 c. powdered sugar
zest of 1/2 an orange
orange juice
Garnish: chocolate sprinkles,
   candied fruit and red and
   green cherries

Cream together shortening and sugar. Add egg and beat well. Sift together flour, baking powder and salt. Add to the sugar mixture alternately with the mashed carrots. Drop by teaspoonfuls onto a greased cookie sheet. Bake at 350 degrees for 15 to 20 minutes, depending on size. The cookies will be firm and orange when baked but not browned. Combine powdered sugar and orange zest. Add enough orange juice until icing spreads easily. Frost cookies after they have completely cooled. Decorate with chocolate sprinkles, candied fruit and red and green cherries.

✳ *Look for vintage cookie jars all year 'round at tag sales or flea markets. Filled with your favorite cookies, brownies and candy, they'll make great gifts for friends and neighbors...along with all the goodies inside!*

Chocolate Crinkle Cookies

Marissa Charytan
North Bellmore, NY

If you like chocolate, you'll love these, and they're so pretty, too!

1/2 c. oil	2 t. vanilla extract
4 1-oz. squares unsweetened chocolate, melted	1/2 t. salt
	2 c. all-purpose flour
2 c. sugar	2 t. baking powder
4 ex. lg. eggs	1 c. powdered sugar

Mix oil, chocolate and sugar. Add one egg at a time until well mixed. Add vanilla, salt, flour and baking powder. Chill overnight, or for several hours. Heat oven to 350 degrees. Shape dough into balls of about one teaspoon each and roll in powdered sugar. Place dough balls approximately 2 inches apart on a well greased baking sheet. Bake 10 to 12 minutes. Makes about 50 cookies.

'Tis Christmas morning:
Christmas mirth,
and joyous voices
fill the house.

-Thomas Bailey Aldrich

Brown Sugar Crackles

Kim Goggin
Denver, CO

Spicy cookies like these are perfect with a glass of icy cold milk.

2 c. brown sugar, packed
1/4 c. butter, softened
1/4 c. oil
2 eggs
2 t. vanilla extract

2 c. all-purpose flour
2/3 c. whole wheat flour
1 t. baking powder
1 t. salt

Cream brown sugar, butter, oil, eggs and vanilla. Stir in dry ingredients. Divide the dough in half and roll out on a floured surface to 1/4-inch thickness. Cut out cookies with round 2-inch cookie cutter and place on a lightly oiled cookie sheet. Bake at 350 degrees for 8 to 10 minutes; until puffed in the center and browned on the edges. Let stand for 2 minutes and remove to rack to cool.

Everyone can know the special magic of waiting for St. Nick on Christmas Eve. Everyone can be a child at Christmas; all we have to do is just believe.

-Anonymous

Desserts

Old English Steamed Pudding

April Jacobs
Loveland, CO

You'll need a pudding steamer for this old-fashioned recipe, but it's well worth the extra effort!

1/2 c. beef suet, chopped
2-2/3 c. dry bread crumbs
1 c. carrots, grated
4 eggs, separated and divided
1-1/3 c. brown sugar, packed
zest of one lemon
1 T. vinegar

2 T. all-purpose flour
1 t. salt
1 t. cinnamon
1/2 t. nutmeg
1/4 t. ground cloves
1-3/4 c. raisins

Beat suet with a heavy-duty mixer until creamy. Blend in bread crumbs and carrots; mixing well. Beat egg yolks until light, add brown sugar and continue to beat until smooth; blend into suet. Stir in lemon zest and vinegar. Sift together flour, salt, cinnamon, nutmeg, cloves and raisins; add to suet mixture. Beat egg whites until stiff and add 1/3 into the pudding mixture. Stir gently, then fold in remaining egg whites until well blended. Spoon pudding into a well buttered 2-quart pudding steamer with a tight fitting lid. Fill the steamer no more than 2/3 full and close lid. Place a canning rack in the bottom of a large pot or water bath canner, this will allow water to circulate round the steamer. Add water to the pot to cover the steamer halfway up its sides. Bring the water to a boil, then place the steamer on the rack and cover the water bath canner or pot. Allow water to boil gently for 3-1/2 hours. Remove steamer and cool for 10 minutes before opening.

Hard Sauce:

5 T. butter
1 c. powdered sugar

1/2 t. vanilla extract

Cream butter, slowly add powdered sugar. Add vanilla and blend well. Spoon over warm pudding.

Spicy Cake Donuts

Liz Roundtree
Petersburg, AK

We enjoy this after a trip of sledding or snowmobiling served with warm apple cider, cocoa or cinnamon tea.

3-1/4 c. all-purpose flour
2 t. baking powder
1-1/2 t. cinnamon, divided
1/4 t. salt
2 eggs

1-1/4 c. sugar, divided
1 t. vanilla extract
2/3 c. light cream
1/4 c. butter, melted

Combine flour, baking powder, one teaspoon cinnamon and salt. Beat together eggs, 2/3 cup sugar and vanilla until thick and lemon colored. Combine cream and butter. Alternate dry ingredients and cream mixture to egg mixture. Beat each time until just blended. Chill dough for 2 hours. Roll out dough 3/8-inch thick on a powdered sugar or floured surface. Cut with donut cutter. Fry in 375 degree oil turning once; allow about one minute per side. Drain on paper towels. Shake warm donuts in small brown bag with remaining sugar and cinnamon. Makes approximately 20 donuts.

❄ *A little red wagon, sled or sleigh looks wonderful on your porch all winter long! Fill them with greenery, holly pine cones, mistletoe and bundles of cinnamon sticks.*

Desserts

Creamy Fudge

Karen Slack
Mt. Pleasant, TX

This is the most creamy and delicious fudge!

1 lb. butter
1 lb. pasteurized process cheese
   spread
4 lbs. powdered sugar

1 c. cocoa
1 t. vanilla extract
2 c. nuts, chopped

In saucepan, melt butter and cheese. Sift together powdered sugar and cocoa. Add cheese and butter mixture, blend completely. Add vanilla and nuts. Mix well and divide evenly between oiled 13"x9" and oiled 8" square baking pans. Spread evenly, cool and cut into small squares. Makes 6-1/2 pounds of fudge.

Windowboxes aren't just for warm weather! This winter fill them with boughs of greenery, pine cones, sleigh bells, apples and pineapples. Tuck in sprigs of mistletoe, holly and colorful lights, too.

Easy Cheesecake

Pam Hilton
Centerburg, OH

A yummy microwave recipe!

1/4 c. butter, melted
1 c. graham cracker crumbs
2/3 c. plus 2 T. sugar, divided
2 8-oz. pkgs. cream cheese
1/4 t. salt

1/3 c. milk
4 eggs
2 T. lemon juice
Garnish: 1 c. sour cream or
1 c. cherry pie filling

Place butter in a 9" glass pie plate. Stir in crumbs and 2 tablespoons sugar; mix well. Press evenly in bottom of dish. Microwave on high for 1-1/2 minutes. Place cream cheese in medium mixing bowl. Microwave at 50% for one minute, or until soft. Add remaining sugar, salt and milk. Beat at medium speed with an electric mixer until blended. Beat in eggs and lemon juice. Microwave on high for 4 to 7 minutes, or until very hot; pour mixture over crust. Microwave at 50% for 7 to 15 minutes, or until almost set in center. Cool slightly. Spread with desired topping. Refrigerate at least 8 hours before serving. Makes 8 to 10 servings.

✳ *A criss-crossed pair of snowshoes makes a fun wintertime welcome! Look for them at flea markets and tag sales. Just cross a pair and secure with heavy-duty wire; don't forget to make a loop in the back for hanging. Hide the wire with bunches of greenery and hang on your front door!*

Desserts

Snowball Cake

Marian Buckley
Fontana, CA

*When the winter winds blow and the January snow is
deep, make this special treat for your family.*

2 3-oz. pkgs. unflavored gelatin
1/8 to 1/4 c. cold water
1 c. boiling water
1 c. sugar
15-1/4 oz. can crushed
    pineapple
juice of one lemon
2 c. whipped topping, divided
1 angel food cake
Garnish: 7 oz. flaked coconut
    and 6-oz. jar maraschino
    cherries

Soften gelatin in cold water; add boiling water and dissolve. Add sugar, pineapple, lemon juice and chill until thick. Fold in one cup whipped topping. Line 13"x9" pan with wax paper. Cut angel food cake into small pieces. Place alternate layers of gelatin mix and cake until all is used. Chill overnight. Spread with remaining whipped topping and place coconut and cherries on top.

Christmas Cups

Wendy Paffenroth
Pine Island, NY

I made this 5 times during the holidays!

12-oz. bag chocolate chips
2 T. butter
14-oz. can sweetened condensed
    milk
14 oz. flaked coconut
1/2 c. walnuts

In a microwave-safe bowl, combine chocolate chips and butter. Heat on low power until melted; stir to blend in butter. Combine condensed milk and coconut; stir until blended. Place candy papers on tray. Place a teaspoonful of chocolate in bottom of each paper, layer on the coconut mixture and top with another dollop of chocolate. Add on a walnut and refrigerate until firm. Makes 20 to 30.

WINTER

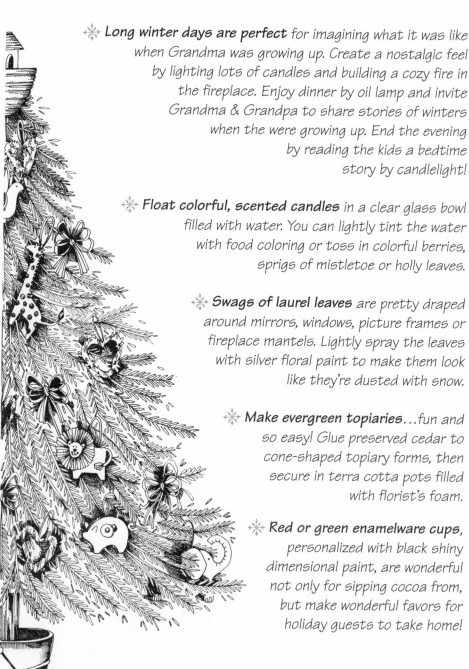

❊ **Long winter days are perfect** for imagining what it was like when Grandma was growing up. Create a nostalgic feel by lighting lots of candles and building a cozy fire in the fireplace. Enjoy dinner by oil lamp and invite Grandma & Grandpa to share stories of winters when the were growing up. End the evening by reading the kids a bedtime story by candlelight!

❊ **Float colorful, scented candles** in a clear glass bowl filled with water. You can lightly tint the water with food coloring or toss in colorful berries, sprigs of mistletoe or holly leaves.

❊ **Swags of laurel leaves** are pretty draped around mirrors, windows, picture frames or fireplace mantels. Lightly spray the leaves with silver floral paint to make them look like they're dusted with snow.

❊ **Make evergreen topiaries**...fun and so easy! Glue preserved cedar to cone-shaped topiary forms, then secure in terra cotta pots filled with florist's foam.

❊ **Red or green enamelware cups**, personalized with black shiny dimensional paint, are wonderful not only for sipping cocoa from, but make wonderful favors for holiday guests to take home!

✳ **A terra cotta pot**, large or small, looks wonderful filled with a beeswax votive or pillar sitting inside. They look especially pretty paired with paper bag luminarias.

✳ **Make nostalgic cards or gift tags** from color copies of favorite photos; sepia tone or black and white copies look best. Using heavy card stock, decide the size you'd like and cut using decorative-edging scissors. In the middle of your tag, cut out a square or oval and use a glue stick to attach a slightly larger square of vellum to cover the opening. Lay your color copy, face down, behind the vellum and glue in place. Add ribbon loops for hanging.

✳ **A pine cone swag** will stay fresh all winter long! Just attach large pine cones to an evergreen wreath using heavy wire. Cover almost all the greenery then pull out several sprigs, letting them peek through the pine cones.

✳ **An heirloom tree skirt** can easily be stitched together with scraps of old quilts, homespun, outgrown dresses and fabric yo-yos...a family keepsake to cherish.

snowflakes gingerbread wreaths family memories candlelight snowmen choirs singing crazy layers evergreens hot cocoa fireside glow giving gifts snowflakes gingerbread wreaths family memories candlelight snowmen crazy layers choirs singing evergreens hot cocoa

Index

Index

Index